BACKROADS

—— *of* ——

NEW ENGLAND

BACKROADS

—————— of ——————

NEW ENGLAND

Your Guide to New England's Most Scenic Backroad Adventures

Text by Kim Knox Beckius
Photography by William H. Johnson

Voyageur Press

A Pictorial
Discovery Guide

DEDICATION

To my wife, Marilyn, the love of my life
—WHJ

To Lara, who traveled some of these roads on the inside and some on the outside
—KKB

Edited by Josh Leventhal
Designed by Andrea Rud
Maps designed by Mary Firth
Printed in China

04 05 06 07 08   5 4 3 2 1

Library of Congress Cataloging-in-Publication Data

Beckius, Kim Knox.
  Backroads of New England : your guide to New England's most scenic backroad adventures
    / text by Kim Knox Beckius; photography by William H. Johnson.
      p. cm. — (A pictorial discovery guide)
  Includes bibliographical references and index.
  ISBN 0-89658-608-1 (pbk.)
 1. New England—Guidebooks. 2. Automobile travel—New England—Guidebooks.
    3. Scenic byways—New England—Guidebooks.
I. Title. II. Series.
  F2.3.B425 2004
  917.404′44—dc22

2004009376

Published by Voyageur Press, Inc.
123 North Second Street, P.O. Box 338, Stillwater, MN 55082 U.S.A.
651-430-2210, fax 651-430-2211
books@voyageurpress.com
www.voyageurpress.com

Educators, fundraisers, premium and gift buyers, publicists, and marketing managers: Looking for creative products and new sales ideas? Voyageur Press books are available at special discounts when purchased in quantities, and special editions can be created to your specifications. For details contact the marketing department at 800-888-9653.

On the front cover: *West Arlington Covered Bridge, West Arlington, Vermont. On the back cover: (top) Bass Head Harbor Light, Acadia National Park, Maine; (bottom left) red maples and sugar maples in fall, Hillsborough Center, New Hampshire; (bottom right) Henry Whitfield House, Guilford, Connecticut.*

Title page: *Rhode Island's Beavertail Light is one of many distinctive beacons standing guard over New England's scenic coastline.*

Title page, inset: *Country paths such as this one in Massachusetts's Berkshire County provide intimate encounters with New England's famous fall foliage.*

CONTENTS

INTRODUCTION

Facing page: *The peaks of Mount Mansfield offer a distinctive backdrop to the farms of northern Vermont's Lamoille River Valley.*

Above: *History abounds throughout New England. This restored Rhode Island mill dates back to 1662.*

You will not find photos of New England in this book. New England is more aura than tangible locale, a blend of people and places bound by history, mythology, geography, and purpose. No single image can adequately convey the region's mystique or the infinite diversity of its visual appeal. Even if one snapshot could honestly portray New England's essence, it would be all wrong three months later when a new season's colors are unveiled.

What you will find are breathtaking images of Connecticut, Rhode Island, Massachusetts, Vermont, New Hampshire, and Maine, the six deeply individual states that historically and geographically compose the place we call New England. Although these states sacrifice a smidge of their unique identities in belonging to the regional whole, each could hold its own in a boasting contest with the best of the other forty-four.

We hope these incomparable New England sights and behind-the-scenes stories will inspire you to drive New England for the first time or the fiftieth. Maps, directions, and tips will help you to navigate some of the most wondrous areas within each state.

The thirty routes were selected to give armchair and on-road travelers a sense of the distinctive and alluring beauty found within this diverse region. Care has been taken to select routes in each of the six states and within many regions of each state. All of New England's remarkable vistas—from ocean swells to tranquil lakes, mountain ranges to fertile lowlands, preserved wild expanses to cultivated gardens and farms, natural formations to historic structures—are represented.

We have attempted to strike a balance between classic, well-traveled New England scenic routes and out-of-the-way drives that may be little known, even to native New Englanders. Each could easily serve as the core of a day's outing. In many cases, we have recommended additional roads, should your day's drive whet your appetite for more of New England's visual splendor. Whether you travel by motorcycle, sporty convertible, family sedan, or SUV, most of these roads are accessible, though weather and road conditions should always be taken into consideration. Vehicle limitations, where they exist, are indicated.

Roads were rather haphazardly designed in early New England, and though few of the former foot trails and cowpaths remain unpaved, many still follow circuitous and unpredictable lines. A compass and additional maps are never a bad idea. Frequent stops will allow you to appreciate the landscape at a slower pace and to check with locals that you're on the track you anticipated.

We realize that for every route we have selected, another deserves equal consideration. Short of pacing around hoping for a sequel to this guide, there is much you can do if backroads are in your blood. In fact, it's typical Yankee operating procedure to take matters into your own hands and find additional byways that beckon to you. The only quintessential image of New England is the vivid and deeply personal montage that resides in your mind and your heart.

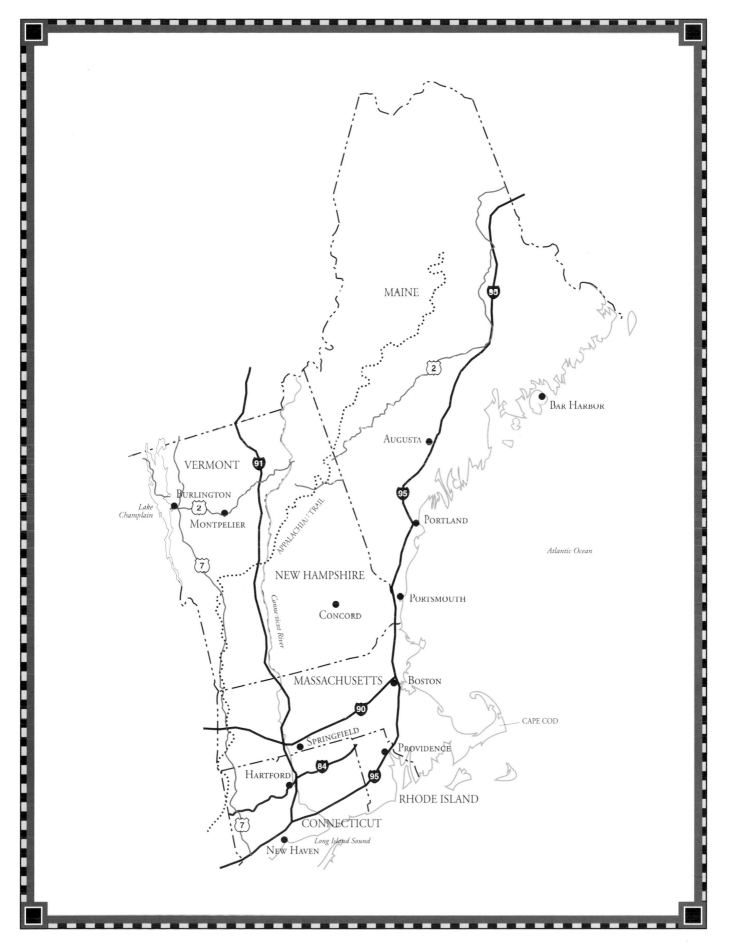

MAINE

95

2

Bar Harbor

Augusta

VERMONT

91

95

Portland

Burlington

Lake
Champlain

2

Montpelier

Atlantic Ocean

7

NEW HAMPSHIRE

Portsmouth

Connecticut River

APPALACHIAN TRAIL

Concord

MASSACHUSETTS

Boston

CAPE COD

90

Springfield

Providence

84

Hartford

95

RHODE ISLAND

7

CONNECTICUT

Long Island Sound

New Haven

Above:
This red sugar maple and old stone wall in Litchfield County, Connecticut, provide a classic New England autumn scene.

Right:
New Hampshire's Kancamagus Highway is a prime leaf-peeping route, one of the best in all of New England.

Left: *Vibrant maples frame the steeple of Ashfield's meeting house in western Massachusetts.*

Below: *Reds, oranges, and yellows illuminate the banks of Salmon Falls River, another autumn gem in the Berkshires of Massachusetts.*

Autumn is by far the favored season for scenic driving in New England. More important than the absence of snow and ice, mud and bugs, and heat and humidity is the dependable annual arrival of fall colors. Mother Nature can be counted on for a consistent palette of fierce reds, dazzling golds, and vivid corals and for her propensity to paint from the top of the canvas downward, gracing the northern forests of Maine, New Hampshire, and Vermont with the first subtle shadings and adding the final daubs of color to the Connecticut coast and Cape Cod.

That's about where her predictability ends, though. You see, Mother Nature is also a mischievous scientist, and each year she tweaks the variables that influence the progression of the season—sunlight, wind, precipitation, temperature. The result is a maddening uncertainty for would-be leaf peepers, who need to make travel decisions months before the gallery reveals opening and closing dates for the year's biggest show. As a rule, color can be found somewhere in New England from about the third week of September through the end of October, but predicting when any given spot will reach its peak is practically impossible.

Chasing the leaves is an option, and once the season is underway, the region's tourism offices help peepers pinpoint peak spots with regular foliage reports. A better strategy is to renounce dependence on the leaves' cooperation and embrace, instead, the full experience of autumn in New England. It is a multi-sensory adventure, and while hills, mountains, and river valleys resplendent with autumn tints are a key component, it is a privilege to exist amid this work in progress, even if the leaves are just starting to turn or have already abandoned their posts. The sweet yet tart taste of fresh-pressed cider, the snapping and crackling of leaves beneath your feet, and the chill-chasing warmth provided by late afternoon sunshine or glowing fireplace embers add sensual dimensions every bit as memorable as spying the spectacle of foliage's vibrant decline.

Almost every New England road can be a leaf-peeping route when the timing is right, but some drives are particularly renowned for spectacular autumn vistas. In Connecticut, the Litchfield Hills and the northeastern Quiet Corner offer the loveliest leaf scenes. In Rhode Island, opt for the inland route through the Arcadia Management Area. Western Massachusetts has that state's best reputation for fall colors, and the Mohawk Trail is a cherished foliage drive. All the Vermont routes offer foliage-viewing possibilities, so select a destination based on the timing of your visit. Many say that the Kancamagus Highway is not just New Hampshire's best autumn drive but the most picturesque foliage route in all of New England. The vastness of Maine makes timing key, but for ultimate drama, head west to the mountains and lakes region.

The changing of the leaves is a dynamic process, and each meticulously pigmented specimen is a singular work, so it is impossible to ever see the entirety of Mother Nature's artistry. Autumn always fades too fast, but amid all the vagaries of life, it is reassuring to know that the temperamental, experimental artist will pick up her paints again next year.

WHY DO LEAVES CHANGE COLOR?

New England's autumn scenery is not just a sight for the eyes, it also provides an intriguing science lesson. As you motor along tree-lined lanes in September and October, take a moment to ponder the rather amazing process by which trees become the region's prime tourist attraction.

For starters, it is important to understand why leaves are green in the first place. Green plants have an ability that is unique in the natural world—they make their own food. The glucose or sugar that sustains plants and trees is manufactured from carbon dioxide and water via a chemical process known as photosynthesis, and the byproduct, of course, is the oxygen that sustains most other life forms, including leaf peepers. Chlorophyll, a green pigment in leaf cells, plays a vital role in this process, as it absorbs the sunlight that powers photosynthesis.

Chlorophyll is not the only pigment in leaves, however. It is simply the most dominant when summer shines. Carotenoids, those pigments responsible for yellow, orange, and brown shades, are there all along. As days shorten, hours of sunlight diminish, and the process of photosynthesis slows to a halt. The result is that the colors masked by chlorophyll are gradually unveiled. In other words, tree leaves don't actually turn yellow or orange, they simply become less green.

Some trees also make pigments known as anthocyanins, which are responsible for red and purple hues. Unlike carotenoids, these pigments are not naturally present in leaves. Instead, anthocyanins are produced only when certain conditions are present, namely when autumn days are warm and sunny and nights are chilly but not freezing. Under these conditions, leaves produce sugar by day, but at night, cold impedes the movement of the synthesized sugar through the leaf's veins and on to the tree's branches and trunk. Anthocyanins are produced as sugar levels build up in leaves, and these pigments either blend with or overpower carotenoids to produce rich coral and crimson tints.

Thus, although the number of sunlight hours has the most direct impact on the onset and intensity of leaves' annual changeover, temperature and other factors also play a role. In addition, drought conditions can force leaves into a premature state of dormancy, and heavy winds can wrest them from their branches before the pigment parade gets fully underway.

New England is far from the only place where leaves try on a new wardrobe before their farewell performance, so why is the region so revered for its radiant autumn splendor? The answer lies primarily in the dense clumps of singular tree species that exist on the sides of mountain slopes and along silvery lakeshores. As stands of like trees—oaks, maples, birch, and others—experience the onslaught of shorter days and colder temperatures together, they tend to don a consistent uniform. The result is thick, lush color clusters that seldom fail to impress.

Though science is truly the force behind New England's most brilliant season, each leaf specimen that twirls to the hardening ground is an original work of art. As you roam the region's backroads, collect a few and press them between the pages of a book. They will remind you that the true test of leaf appreciation is heeding the call to return to New England's autumn spectacle year after year.

PART I

CONNECTICUT: TRUE COLORS

Facing page: *The fiery colors of autumn jolt sleepy towns such as Woodstock, Connecticut, out of their yesteryear slumber.*

Above: *Town greens are enduring symbols of community throughout New England. Connecticut boasts more than 150, including the densely treed, triangular green in the town of Branford.*

Diamonds are created under great heat and pressure. Squeezed between New York and Massachusetts, Connecticut is a gem whose most brilliant facets are easily overlooked. Many travelers simply cut through Connecticut along nondescript interstates. Thousands marvel at the manmade waterfall inside the Mohegan Sun Casino yet never set eyes on more striking falls fashioned by nature. Cutting away from the highways is clearly the route to Connecticut's true colors.

Connecticut, the third smallest state in America, ranks among the nation's most densely populated. Still, the rural northeastern region earns its "Quiet Corner" nickname. The Litchfield Hills harbor vineyards and forest preserves. Even along Long Island Sound and the Connecticut River, where 90 percent of the state's residents are clustered, sleepy villages reverberate with character from colonial origins and maritime glory days.

Connecticut's modern affluence is tied largely to its wealthiest citizens' New York City paychecks. Its history, though, is closely linked to its Yankee compatriots. The Constitution State acts like a prism, diffusing the bright lights of the big city into the soft spectrum of New England hues. Once you leave the commuter-clogged highways for seaside causeways and tree-shaded country lanes, you will encounter stone walls, town greens, covered bridges, river ferries, island sanctuaries, and snug seaports that leave no doubt that this jewel is properly set.

UNEXPECTED CONNECTICUT
THE LITCHFIELD HILLS AND
THE HOUSATONIC RIVER VALLEY

Envision whitewater rafting in New England and you probably first think of Maine. Vermont may be the most likely destination for skiing or fly-fishing. Following in the footsteps of George Washington might mean Massachusetts, and a covered bridge quest could take you to New Hampshire. For chichi shops, Boston and Newport likely come to mind. Then again, you can find all of this in northwestern Connecticut.

A day's drive through the southern foothills of the Berkshire Mountains will introduce you to facets of Connecticut's personality frequently overlooked by travelers who assume they need to journey farther north to find the "real" New England. Lovely Litchfield County is a bit like an appetizer sampler platter that leaves you wondering why you bothered to order an entrée.

The hilltop town of Litchfield alone may satisfy your hunger for the flavor of old New England, spiced with cosmopolitan flair. The town green, now ringed with upscale boutiques and restaurants that attract celebrity clientele, dates to 1723, just two years after the first settlers arrived. Litchfield's protected inland location allowed it to prosper during the American Revolution, when it served as a supply stop and munitions storehouse for Washington's Continental Army. At the northeast end of the

ROUTE 1

From Litchfield, follow Route 63 North to the rotary in Goshen. Go three-quarters of the way around the rotary and turn right onto Route 4 West. Turn left at a stop sign to stay on Route 4 West. In Cornwall Bridge, take Route 7 North to a right on Route 128 East. Drive across the West Cornwall Covered Bridge, make a U-turn, and return to Route 7 South. Stay on Route 7 through Kent. Turn right on Bulls Bridge Road, drive across the Bulls Bridge covered bridge, reverse, and return to Route 7 North back to Kent. Turn right onto Route 341 East, and after Route 341 joins Route 45 South, watch for a right turn to stay on Route 45 when the roads split. In New Preston, turn left on Route 202 East to Litchfield.

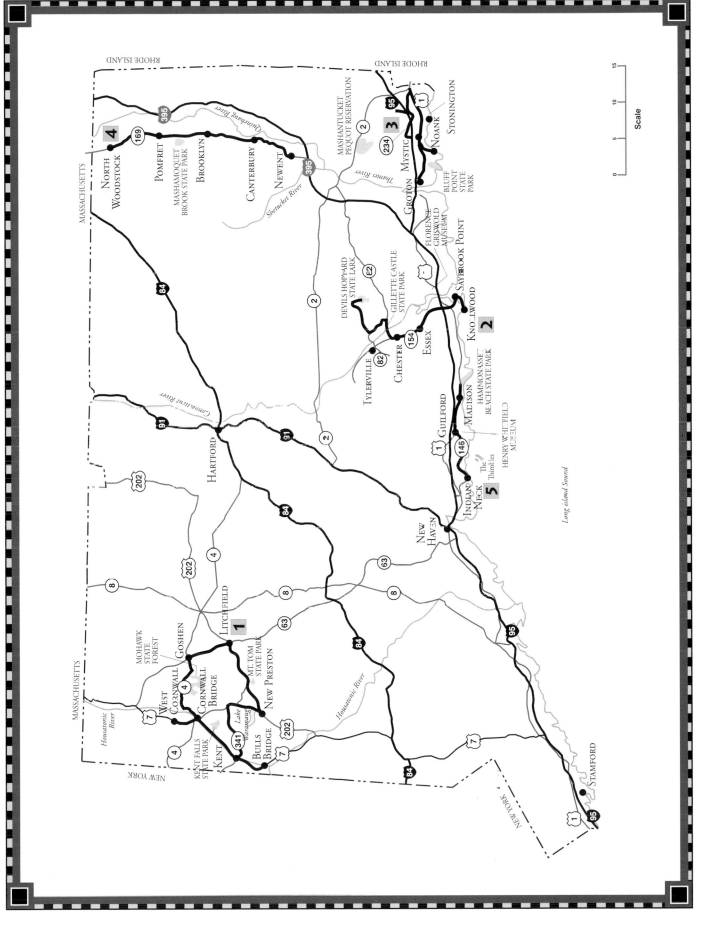

Left: *The landmark First Congregational Church anchors the northeast side of the town green in Litchfield, a quintessential New England town with appeal that is as perennial as the dandelions that poke their sunny heads up each spring.*

Left: *The gently sloping Litchfield Hills provide diverse vantage points from which to appreciate the lush hues of autumn.*

Above: *Winter is a quiet and contemplative time to discover the surprisingly rural charm of northwestern Connecticut.*

green, you'll notice the landmark First Congregational Church, a Greek revival–style structure built in 1829 as the third meetinghouse for a growing congregation.

Though industry declined in Litchfield by the 1830s, the town's resurgence as a resort community began in the latter part of that century. Today, historic sites such as America's first law school at the Tapping Reeve House continue to draw visitors. Colonial homes have been snatched up by urban transplants and weekenders, who inject the historic village with an uncommon level of sophistication.

Once you have strolled the tree-lined streets of Litchfield, head north toward Goshen, site of the Connecticut Agricultural Fair each July. From Route 63, a spin around the rotary in Goshen places you on Route 4 West, which will take you to the first of four state parks along this meandering route. In Cornwall, watch for the Mohawk State Forest entrance on the left. Explore the trails within this 2,900-acre wooded wildlife sanctuary, which features a preserved black spruce bog and a lookout tower. The entrance to Mohawk Mountain, Connecticut's oldest ski area, is just a bit farther west. Would you have guessed that commercial snowmaking made its debut in Connecticut? In 1949, ski mogul Walt Schoenknecht gave Mother Nature a boost by developing the first commercial-grade snow gun at his Connecticut ski resort. That same year, he discovered the next mountain he would eventually claim for New England skiers—Vermont's Mount Snow.

When you reach Cornwall Bridge, bear right and follow Route 7 along the banks of the Housatonic, a swift, narrow river capable of Class V rapids. You'll likely see rafters, kayakers, and waist-deep fly fishermen casting for trout and bass as you pass Housatonic Meadows State Park. Here, many outdoor enthusiasts pitch tents under towering pines. Campers include hikers navigating the stretch of the Appalachian Trail that runs along the river.

A brief detour onto Route 128 will take you to the West Cornwall Covered Bridge. Yes, Connecticut has covered bridges, and the West Cornwall span is one of only two covered bridges in the state that are open to vehicular traffic. You will encounter the other one shortly, but first you'll need to reverse direction and drive south through the town of Kent. Several attractions will entice you to reach for your blinker, beginning with the dramatic cascade at Kent Falls State Park. In the park, you can picnic beside the falls and stroll through a 1974 reproduction covered bridge. Keep in mind that you are seeing only the final 70-foot plummet of this 250-foot series of falls.

Farther south on Route 7, the seasonally operated Sloane-Stanley Museum showcases early American tools collected by Connecticut artist and writer Eric Sloane. Kent also offers eclectic shopping and dining diversions, but press on south of town to Bulls Bridge Road and drive across the 1842 covered bridge over the Housatonic River. At this site, George

Washington crossed an earlier bridge when it was still under construction. How do we know? His expense account statement of March 3, 1781, includes the entry, "Getting a horse out of Bulls Bridge Falls, $215."

Your car isn't likely to suffer a similar fate, which is good considering the return trip to Litchfield still includes a few tantalizing sights, such as the serene waters of Lake Waramaug. On North Shore Road, you'll find the lake's only public swimming and boating access within Lake Waramaug State Park. Nearby, a lakeshore winery, Hopkins Vineyard, offers tours and tastings. The vineyard's loft is a perfect place from which to view autumn hues mirrored in Lake Waramaug's still waters.

Follow the lake's eastern shore to New Preston, where shops clustered within the cute village center range from antique to chic. Route 202 East will speed you back to Litchfield—unless you're up for a few more stops. Mount Tom State Park offers a swimming and ice-skating pond; a one-mile trail leads to a three-story stone lookout tower with incomparable views of the region's rolling hills. Just before you find yourself back in the heart of Litchfield, stop at the White Memorial Conservation Center, the state's largest wildlife preserve. It has a nature museum, 35 miles of trails, a campground, and boating facilities.

You probably won't have time to savor all of the hidden delights of Litchfield County during one day's drive, but now that you've had a sampling, you'll know exactly where to go the next time you crave a taste of New England.

Below: *The town of Litchfield in northwestern Connecticut blends old-time charm with contemporary style. The county courthouse, dating to 1889, anchors the town's main thoroughfare. (Photograph by William H. Johnson)*

Overleaf: *The waters of New England's longest river, the Connecticut, have flowed nearly 400 miles from their origin by the time they reach East Haddam as the light of day subsides.*

BETWEEN THE DEVIL AND THE SHALLOW BLUE SEA
THE CONNECTICUT RIVER VALLEY

From Knollwood Beach, follow Route 154 East to Saybrook Point and then Route 154 North through the town of Old Saybrook. Turn right onto West Avenue and, at the rotary, go straight on Main Street to the village of Essex. Return to Route 154 and head north to a right turn on Route 148 East. Cross the Connecticut River via the Chester-Hadlyme Ferry (operates seasonally). On the river's eastern shore, continue on Route 148 East, then bear left onto Geer Hill Road, which becomes River Road, following signs to Gillette Castle State Park. On exiting the castle, turn left on River Road, then left onto Route 82 West. In East Haddam, turn right on Mount Parnassus Road, which becomes Millington Road, then Haywardville Road. Turn right onto Hopyard Road to Devil's Hopyard State Park. *Note: When the ferry is not in operation, follow Route 154 North all the way to Route 82 East at Tylerville. Turn right onto River Road to Gillette Castle, then resume following the directions above.*

You can't wriggle your toes in the sand at the members-only Knollwood Beach. Nor can you drive into Fenwick, the luxurious, seaside gated community that was home to screen legend Katharine Hepburn. There's nothing, though, to keep you from stealing a glance at the elite views as you cruise east along the Long Island Sound on Route 154. One hundred miles long but only 21 miles across at its widest point, the sound is an ocean tease. The saltwater inlet averages only 65 feet in depth, but these waters run deep when it comes to their impact on Connecticut history.

Offshore, the Saybrook Breakwater Light illuminates the entrance to an even more influential waterway, the Connecticut River. The white cast-iron lighthouse, also known as Saybrook Outer Light, was erected in 1886. The Inner Light, or Lynde Point Light, dates back even earlier, to 1838, but it is less easily viewed due to its location onshore at the end of a private Fenwick road. Neither lighthouse is open to the public, and both remain active aids to navigation, marking the mouth of New England's longest river. First explored by Dutch navigator Adriaen Block in 1614, the Connecticut River was key to the Europeans' conquest of inland New England. By 1633, fertile lands had attracted English settlers to valley towns near present-day Hartford, some 40 miles upriver. In 1635, Old Saybrook became the first colonial outpost on the state's southern shore.

Head north from Saybrook Point and leave the sea behind for a trek along this historic river. As you leave the point, watch for the entrance to Fort Saybrook Monument Park on the right. Connecticut's first military fortifications were built on this site by English settlers, who battled the Dutch and the Pequots for control of the point.

Route 154 becomes Old Saybrook's bustling Main Street; commercial development largely cloaks the town's colonial origins. Essex, however, is one of New England's best-preserved pre-Revolution towns, and here you'll be rewarded with the opportunity to learn more about the *Quonitocutt*, or "Long Tidal River," as it was called by native peoples.

Settled in 1648, Essex was a wealthy shipbuilding and seafaring mecca by the mid eighteenth century. The exquisite former homes of boat builders, merchants, and sea captains line Main Street, along with an assortment of shops. For a blast from the past, dine at the Griswold Inn, which has offered warm hospitality to travelers and locals alike since 1776. Main Street dead-ends at the riverfront, where you'll discover the Connecticut River Museum housed in an 1878 steamboat warehouse. Among its most intriguing exhibits is a working reproduction of the world's first submarine, the *American Turtle*. Designed and built by David Bushnell of Old

Saybrook, the craft was devised to be the colonists' "secret weapon" in the war for independence.

It's time for a more intimate encounter with the Connecticut. Wind your way past Deep River's antique shops to Chester, where Route 148 East would lead you straight into the river were it not for the historic ferry awaiting your arrival. In operation since 1769 and now under the jurisdiction of the Connecticut Department of Transportation, the Chester-Hadlyme Ferry offers quick, affordable transport across the Connecticut from April through November. Be sure to hop out of your car during this short trip to catch the dramatic views of the river and the castle perched high above it.

Surprised to see a German-style medieval castle on the banks of the Connecticut? You wouldn't be if you'd known the rather eccentric Hartford native William Gillette, a successful actor, playwright, and director best known for his portrayals of Sherlock Holmes. The million-dollar castle, completed in 1919, features many peculiarities, including hidden mirrors and forty-seven different intricate, hand-carved door latches. One room is fashioned after Sherlock Holmes' sitting room at 221B Baker Street. Gillette, who died in 1937, stipulated in his will that his castle not fall to "some blithering saphead who has no conception of where he is or with what surrounded." The state acquired the property in 1943. Castle tours are offered from Memorial Day through Columbus Day, and the spectacular grounds are also worth perusing.

Between the devil and the deep blue sea isn't usually an ideal place to be, but this journey from the shallow sound to your final stop—Devil's Hopyard State Park—has watery delights at both ends as well as in between. A short walk in the park brings you to one of the state's most impressive waterfalls—Chapman Falls. How in the devil did the park get its odd name? There are several theories, but the most colorful, likely devised by early settlers to explain this geologic phenomenon, identifies the devil himself as the creator of the rock depressions or "potholes" near the falls. As the old story goes, the devil accidentally got his tail wet in the falls, and this made him so hopping mad that he scorched holes in the stones with his fiery hooves as he scampered away.

Docked at Chester, the steam ferry Emily A. Wright *prepares to carry passengers to Hadlyme on the opposite bank of the Connecticut River. The* Emily Λ. Wright *operated at this key river crossing from 1884 to 1889. (Photograph courtesy of the Connecticut Historical Society, Hartford, Connecticut)*

Located at the mouth of the Connecticut River, Saybrook Point Marina is a bustling waypoint for Long Island Sound boaters by day, but the port calms at moonrise.

Once a bustling river harbor, the Essex Village riverfront is now home to the Connecticut River Museum, celebrating New England's most important river.

A Canada goose stands sentry as a bale of turtles basks on a rock in an Essex pond.

From the parking lot just inside Devil's Hopyard State Park, it is a short and easy hike to view the water-sculpted rocks and dramatic 60-foot cascade known as Chapman Falls.

THE SECOND COLONIZATION OF CONNECTICUT

Connecticut's landscape was permanently altered by the arrival of the first European colonists in 1633. Its landscapes were forever preserved, however, by a second colonization that began in 1899, when Tonalist painter Henry Ward Ranger, fresh from his studies in Europe, arrived on the doorstep of a Georgian-style mansion turned boardinghouse in Old Lyme, Connecticut.

Florence Griswold had decided to accept lodgers as a means of preserving her family homestead. For the ensuing three decades, these lodgers would hardly be ordinary transients, though. Ranger's vision of an art colony modeled on the French Barbizon soon became reality, as others flocked to Old Lyme to capture the inspiring local scenery on canvas while enjoying creative collegiality and the famed hospitality of Miss Florence. With Childe Hassam's arrival in 1903, the colony's artistic focus shifted from Tonalism to Impressionism, and Connecticut emerged as the incubator for the American Impressionist movement.

Now a National Historic Landmark open to the public, the Florence Griswold Museum is both a gallery of works by some of America's finest painters and a place imbued with artistic energy. The brushstrokes that adorn the home's dining room and door panels provide a unique opportunity to view art in the space where it originated.

Resident artists dine on the Griswold House back porch in the early 1900s. They called themselves the "Hot Air Club" because they preferred to eat outside in warm weather. (Some wonder if "hot air" was more a reflection of the content of their lunchtime discussions.) (Photograph courtesy of the Florence Griswold Museum; Lyme Historical Society Archives)

A Rich Lega-sea
The Southeastern Shore

Long Island's sheltering embrace creates calm harbors along Connecticut's southeastern shore, where coastal fishing and farming villages feign peaceful slumber. This sleepy countenance can't mask the region's dramatic seafaring past, however. Today, going to sea usually means cruising in luxury. In the eighteenth and nineteenth centuries, the sea-bound were in pursuit of big business—sometimes as big as a whale.

Although the whaling, sealing, shipbuilding, and fishing industries gave this area its distinctive color, it was farming that drew the first homesteaders to Connecticut's coast from Plymouth Colony. Ample evidence of these agricultural roots exists along the winding, scenic Pequot Trail and Taugwonk Road. Colonial farmhouses are lovingly preserved, and tiger lilies bloom brightly against a backdrop of old stone walls, the product of farmers' efforts to clear fields of the glacial debris. Leading from the head of the Mystic River to what is now Westerly, Rhode Island, the Pequot Trail was known to these early residents as simply "The Road." When it was first blazed in 1669—twenty years after the first settlers arrived in Stonington—it was the lone road in the settlement.

Stonington Vineyards on Taugwonk Road is a worthy detour before turning toward Stonington's shore. Here in the Stonington Uplands, the maritime microclimate mimics that of the Bordeaux region of France. You can sample the vineyard's European-style wines and admire the meticulously groomed aisles of vines, which march toward a backdrop of lush countryside. The area is particularly lovely under the influence of autumn.

ROUTE 3

From Old Mystic, follow Route 27 North to Route 234 East, the Pequot Trail. Where Route 234 turns right, continue straight and follow Taugwonk Road to Stonington Vineyards. Return to Route 234 and head west to a left on Route 1/Stonington Road. Turn right onto Route 1A/Elm Street. Where Route 1A turns right, continue straight on Water Street to Stonington Point. Reverse direction and return to Route 1A West. Turn left on Route 1 West to Mystic. After the drawbridge, turn left on Route 215. To reach Noank, turn left on Mosher Avenue and then left on Main Street. The first right, Pearl Street, leads to the waterfront. Return to Route 215 and continue west to rejoin Route 1 West to Groton. Turn left onto Depot Road, to Bluff Point State Park.

The bascule bridge across the Mystic River on Route 1 has been in operation since 1922. "Bascule" is the French word for "seesaw," and this unique type of drawbridge was patented in 1918 by Thomas E. Brown, who also designed the elevator for the Eiffel Tower. Much like a seesaw, the bridge is opened by the mechanical lowering of huge counterbalancing weights. (Photograph by William H. Johnson)

Above: *Sea captains have set sail from Stonington for centuries, and the coastal village remains home base for the state's last surviving commercial fishing fleet.*

Right: *Inactive since 1889, the granite-walled Stonington Harbor Light has been a museum since 1925. Inside, the Stonington Historical Society exhibits local artifacts, and the tower's circular stairs lead to spectacular views.*

Saltwater inlets and tranquil coves along Connecticut's southeastern shore are perfect paddling grounds for kayakers.

Pastoral scenes, such as this Queen Anne's Lace–dotted hillside in North Woodstock, contribute to northeastern Connecticut's "Quiet Corner" nickname.

The storied village of Stonington Borough, home to Connecticut's last surviving commercial fishing fleet, lies south of the Pequot Trail on the shores of Long Island Sound. Federal- and Greek revival–style mansions, once home to sea captains, grace the narrow streets around Cannon Square. In the square, twin cannons stand as relics of the War of 1812's Battle of Stonington, a skirmish in which the coastal town, with just three cannons and a lot of moxie, fended off the heavy artillery of a British naval squadron. Two centuries later, serene shops and cafés line Water Street as it tapers en route to Stonington Point. There, the now inactive 1840 Stonington Harbor Light is a museum of local history. You can climb to the top of the beacon for panoramic views, or simply sit by the beach and watch the wind ripple waves and sails.

Mystic, the next town to the west, is more commercial and touristy than surrounding shoreline towns. Both of its major attractions could easily occupy you for the better part of a day. Mystic Seaport, North America's largest maritime museum, is a 17-acre living-history complex that re-creates the nineteenth-century boom years of this whaling and shipbuilding hub. The Mystic Aquarium and Institute for Exploration offers fascinating exhibits and programs about marine life and our underwater world. Both attractions are easy hops off this route, but the true backroads connoisseur will breeze through downtown Mystic, pausing only if the Route 1 bascule, or seesaw bridge, is open. The oldest of its kind in the nation, the bridge opens to allow tall ships to continue along the Mystic River.

In the drowsy village of Noank, you can stop to enjoy an ice cream cone from Carson's, the 1907 general store. You can also munch a buttery lobster roll at Abbott's Lobster in the Rough; tourists have been dining alfresco on fresh-caught seafood at this seasonal seafood shanty for more than fifty years. The picnic table–strewn lawn overlooking Fishers Island Sound is an ideal vantage point from which to observe departures and arrivals at Noank Shipyard. Noank might be much different if not for a bit of history. The Mashantucket Pequot tribe was given land in Noank in 1651, following the Pequot War, but it was taken from the tribe in exchange for property in Mashantucket fifteen years later. The Mashantucket Pequot Reservation is now home to the world's largest casino, Foxwoods.

For a picture of how the region might have looked had European settlers not encroached on native lands, visit Bluff Point State Park and Coastal Reserve, located in Groton. Established on a $1\frac{1}{2}$-mile wooded peninsula jutting into Fishers Island Sound, the 800-acre protected habitat is the largest undeveloped parcel along Connecticut's coastline. The park is a popular site for kayaking, hiking, wildlife viewing, and sunbathing on the tombolo or sandbar. Your car will have to snooze while you explore, though, as trails are open to non-motorized vehicles and foot traffic only.

CRUISING THE QUIET CORNER
NORTHEAST CONNECTICUT'S
NATIONAL SCENIC BYWAY

ROUTE 4

Follow State Route 169 South from North Woodstock to Newent. Watch for a hard right turn to stay on 169 just past the fairgrounds in Woodstock.

When the U.S. Department of Transportation began designating National Scenic Byways in 1996, Connecticut State Route 169 made the first cut. National Scenic Byways are selected for their archeological, cultural, historic, natural, recreational, or scenic significance. This quiet, tree-lined thoroughfare, which had already been designated a State Scenic Highway in 1991, undoubtedly qualifies on all six counts. The prime leaf-peeping path essentially follows the route of the original Norwich and Woodstock Turnpike, which dates to the 1600s. Now paved and easily navigable, the road bisects the federally designated Quinebaug and Shetucket Rivers Valley National Heritage Corridor in northeastern Connecticut and south-central Massachusetts. This 695,000-acre area is known as "The Last Green Valley," because, in contrast to much of the region between Boston and Washington, D.C., it is uniquely rural and unspoiled.

In order to fully appreciate the character of this drive, you'll want to turn off your cell phone, put away your pager, and hide the GPS unit in the glove compartment—a beep, buzz, or jingle might jolt you out of the yesteryear trance into which this byway will instantly lull you. Route 169, with its stone walls, herb farms, orchards, country fairgrounds, smattering of antique and craft shops, and proliferation of homes built before 1855—an estimated 189 of them—is a worthy diversion from technology's assault on everyday living.

The town of Woodstock was settled in 1686, and to this day, third graders attend class in a one-room schoolhouse, albeit for only one week each spring as they learn about education in bygone days. Pomfret, established in 1686 on land purchased from the Indians for 30 British pounds, was incorporated in 1713. In Mashamoquet Brook State Park, you'll find the Wolf Den, where lore has it that Israel Putnam killed the last wolf in Connecticut—a notorious, sheep-snatching menace—in 1742. He switched from fighting wolves to fighting Redcoats when word arrived of the Battle of Lexington. Putnam, a resident of nearby Brooklyn, left his plow in the field in his rush to join the fight for independence. He would go on to fame as a major general in the Continental Army and is often credited with having uttered the command, "Don't one of you fire until you see

The legend of Israel Putnam has been retold for generations. In this 1830s sketch, two men tell a couple of youngsters the gripping tale of Putnam's encounter with the last Connecticut wolf. An image of a wolf looms in the background above the wolf den. (Photograph courtesy of the Connecticut Historical Society, Hartford, Connecticut)

Above: *When the grounds and formal garden at Roseland Cottage were laid out in 1850, in the style of famed landscape architect Andrew Jackson Downing, the bill from a local nursery for 600 yards of boxwood hedge, flowering and ornamental plants, shrubs, and fruit-bearing trees, plus labor, came to the hefty sum of $550.*

Right: *The Guilford Agricultural Society holds Connecticut's second oldest agricultural fair each year during the third full weekend of September.*

Above: *Located off the coast at Stony Creek, the Thimble Islands retain a mystique and an aura of exclusivity.*

Left: *More than two miles of sand await visitors to Hammonasset Beach State Park in Madison. While some stretches are lined with boardwalks and crowded with bathers, other areas remain protected and pristine.*

the whites of their eyes," at the Battle of Bunker Hill. A monument to the war hero is located in the center of Brooklyn, at 25 Canterbury Street. The Brooklyn Fair, one of the oldest continuously active agricultural fairs in the nation, dates to 1809 and draws visitors to the area each August. The town of Canterbury was first settled in 1690, and its fertile and relatively rock-free land remains home to dairy and other types of farms.

Two National Historic Landmarks along Route 169 are well worth touring when they are open in season. Woodstock's Bowen House, also known as Roseland Cottage, is a Gothic revival–style mansion with Andrew Jackson Downing–inspired gardens and landscaping. Built in 1846, it was the summer home of wealthy Woodstock native and Republican Henry C. Bowen. During his lavish annual Fourth of July parties, Bowen entertained four men who had been, were, or would be president. His house, now operated by Historic New England, is notable for its vibrant sherbet-pink paintjob. Tours include a visit to the home's private bowling alley, where Ulysses S. Grant threw a strike in 1870. The state-operated Prudence Crandall Museum in Can-terbury is the site of the first girls' academy in New England to admit a black woman. Prudence Crandall, who founded the school in 1832, is Connecticut's state heroine, recognized for her staunch perseverance amid the ensuing controversy, which forced the closing of the academy in 1834.

There is more to explore in Connecticut's Quiet Corner, both on and off Route 169, including several vineyards, the antique marketplaces of Putnam, and even a buffalo farm. So there's still no reason to resume the use of your electronic devices. That is, unless you'd like to phone friends to clue them in on the charms of this pristine valley.

BLUES, PINKS, GREENS, AND MAYBE GOLD
CONNECTICUT'S HIDDEN TREASURE COAST

ROUTE 5

From Indian Neck, follow Route 146 East, watching for several turns en route to Guilford. Turn right at the town green in Guilford onto Whitfield Street, then bear left onto Old Whitfield Street. Turn left on Stone House Lane to the Henry Whitfield State Museum. Return to Route 146 East, continuing straight onto Route 1 East. After passing through Madison, enter Hammonasset Beach State Park on the right at a traffic light.

The first sweeping views of Long Island Sound, shimmering silvery blue, pop up abruptly as you set out east from Indian Neck on a winding course through well-preserved shoreline towns with colonial-era origins. While some of the colorful sights along the way require little explanation, a dab of color commentary will help you to integrate the underlying palette of history and intrigue with the canvas framed by your windshield.

You could easily breeze past the archipelago of hundreds of minute isles scattered in Long Island Sound, for example, without realizing that the Thimble Islands were once the stomping grounds of notorious rogue Captain Kidd. You also might not know that the islands are named not for their small size but rather for thimbleberries, a species of raspberry that grows there. Most of the pink granite islands are mere hazards to navigation, but about two dozen are sizable enough to hold from one to a handful of exclusive homes, most built as summertime sanctuaries during the Victorian period. Many of the islands have stories—they're recounted regularly during seasonal boat tours that depart from the town dock in Stony

Creek—but the greatest mystique surrounds the seventeenth-century pirate and the treasure he allegedly stashed in an underwater cave; it's never been found.

The pink granite that has been quarried onshore in Stony Creek for nearly two centuries can be found easily, however. It's been used in New York's Grand Central Station, the Statue of Liberty's pedestal, Battery Park in Lower Manhattan, and the Lincoln Memorial in Washington, D.C. Thimble Islands Road will lead you to Stony Creek's small Willoughby Wallace Memorial Library, which is veneered in the same famous stone.

As Route 146 continues toward Guilford, salt marshes and fieldstone walls are reminders of the challenging terrain early settlers faced when clearing fields for farmland. The Reverend Henry Whitfield led the small band of Puritans who purchased land from the Menuncatuck tribe and in 1639 established Guilford as Connecticut's seventh town. Whitfield's home, touted as Connecticut's oldest extant house and New England's oldest stone house, was acquired by the state in 1900 and became its first state museum. The structure itself has undergone many changes since Whitfield's day, and the eclectic collection it houses makes it more museum than historic home; it is nevertheless a great place to learn about life in colonial Connecticut.

Dozens of other pre-Revolutionary homes survive in Guilford, as does the town's emerald gem—one of New England's largest town greens. At the park-like green, Route 146 becomes Route 1, the old Boston Post Road and still the main thoroughfare through Madison, the next town to the east. Named for President James Madison, the town was part of Guilford until 1826. Madison's more modest town green remains a staging area for community events, and it serves as the "front lawn" for the town's oldest home, the 1685 Deacon John Grave House.

From cozy coffee shops to an independent bookseller to a two-screen cinema, the commercial development along Route 1 in Madison harks back to pre-mall days when downtown districts served as community shopping centers. Many travelers miss Madison's kaleidoscope of shops, though, as they seek the fast track of Interstate 95, heading straight to the blue yonder.

Hammonasset Beach State Park is Connecticut's largest public beach, a 2-mile sandy stretch east of Madison. With its wood-plank boardwalk, picnic pavilions, boat launch, campground, and nature center, Hammonasset has broad appeal, particularly for families who appreciate the tameness of the sound's saltwater surf. Indians who farmed along the banks of the adjoining Hammonassett River gave the area its descriptive name, which means, "where we dig holes in the ground." When summer glows, Hammonasset is still an ideal place for digging holes and building sandcastles. In the off-season, it's a contemplative hideaway, where you can stroll along pink sand dunes, watch green sea grasses bend with the breeze, stare out toward the sapphire sea, and imagine how you'd spend Captain Kidd's gold.

PART II

RHODE ISLAND:
GO YOUR OWN WAY

Facing page: *The night shift is nearly over for Narragansett's Point Judith Light, which has warned sailors away from the Ocean State's rocky coast since 1857.*

Above: *Mattatuxet Brook, an old mill stream, runs alongside the house where prolific portrait painter Gilbert Stuart was born in 1755. Venture inside to see reproductions of some of Stuart's works, or simply fish inside your wallet for a one-dollar bill to see his portrait of George Washington.*

Banished from Massachusetts for his "extremist" views on freedom of speech and religion, Roger Williams founded Rhode Island in 1636 and established America's first truly democratic community. In 1652, Rhode Island enacted the first law abolishing slavery in the New World. Two years before the Boston Tea Party, Rhode Islanders burned the British ship *Gaspee* in Narragansett Bay. On May 4, 1776, a full two months before those pokey patriots in Philadelphia got around to writing and signing a Declaration of Independence, the General Assembly of the Colony of Rhode Island issued its own Renunciation of Allegiance, effectively ending British rule and establishing the state as a free republic. In 1790, Rhode Island became the last of the original colonies to surrender its autonomy and join the fledgling Union. Three years later, Samuel Slater built the first successful textile mill in Pawtucket, touching off America's Industrial Revolution. When the Eighteenth Amendment was added to the United States Constitution in 1919, Rhode Island never ratified Prohibition. It would be odd, after all, for the Ocean State to vote to go dry.

Yes, Rhode Islanders have a long-standing tradition of doing their own thing—if you're unconvinced, just pull over and order some Rhode Island clam chowder. A uniqueness and diversity can be found, too, in the landscape of the nation's smallest state. Along Rhode Island's 400-mile coast, the shore meets the sea in myriad ways, and once you turn inland, unexpected surprises await.

So if Rhode Island's rebellious spirit inspires you to ignore the routes suggested here, that's perfectly okay. Just be sure to keep your eye on your speedometer. Rhode Island was also the first state to arrest a driver and impose a jail sentence for speeding. Of course, that was 1904, and the reckless motorist was racing through Newport at 15 miles per hour.

BEACH-O-DIVERSITY
THE SOUTH COUNTY COAST

Sand is a common denominator, but beyond that grainy surface, the beaches that border Block Island Sound bear little resemblance to one another. From the seaside Victorian charm of Watch Hill to the boisterous beach atmosphere of Misquamicut to the unscathed swath of protected shore within the Ninigret Conservation Area, a day's drive along the Ocean State's southwestern coast reveals the spectrum of possible outcomes wherever land and sea meet.

Situated on a peninsula jutting into the Atlantic, the village of Watch Hill confronts the sea on two sides. Views to the west over Little Narragansett Bay provide an opportunity, rare in New England, to watch the sun sink into the ocean as night falls. In the 1600s, the Niantic Indians occupied this area. A statue commemorating Chief Ninigret is found on Bay Street, the town's main thoroughfare, which is also lined with shops and cafés. Salt-scented breezes tussle little ones' hair as they wait for parents to tire of weaving in and out of the various boutiques. A treat awaits

ROUTE 6

From Watch Hill, head out of town on Bay Street, which becomes Wauwinnet Avenue. Pick up Route 1A North/Shore Road and, at a light, turn right on Winnapaug Road toward Misquamicut Beach. At a stop sign, turn left on Atlantic Avenue, then left onto Weekapaug Road at another stop sign. Turn right at a traffic light and return to Route 1A/Shore Road. When Route 1A ends, bear right onto Route 1 North. Go right on East Beach Road, and when it ends, turn left and follow the dirt access road to the entrance for the Ninigret Conservation Area.

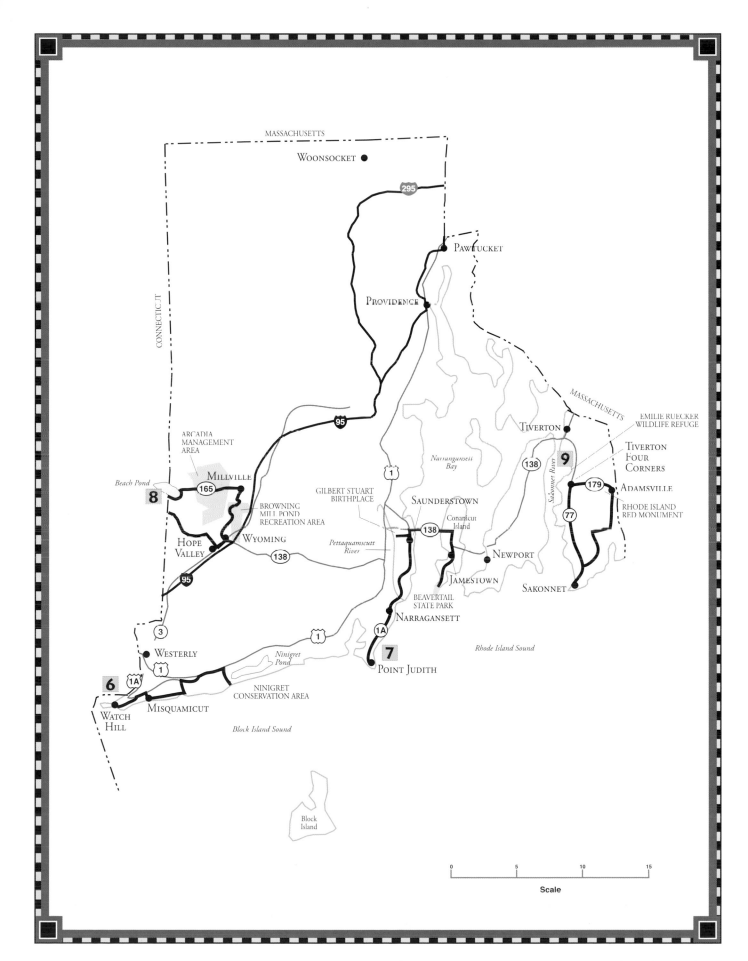

MASSACHUSETTS

WOONSOCKET

295

PAWTUCKET

PROVIDENCE

CONNECTICUT

95

MASSACHUSETTS

ARCADIA
MANAGEMENT
AREA

Beach Pond

MILLVILLE

8

165

BROWNING
MILL POND
RECREATION AREA

HOPE
VALLEY

WYOMING

95

138

3

1

Narragansett
Bay

GILBERT STUART
BIRTHPLACE

SAUNDERSTOWN

Conanicut
Island

138

Pettaquamscutt
River

EMILIE RUECKER
WILDLIFE REFUGE

TIVERTON

138

Sakonnet River

9

179

TIVERTON
FOUR
CORNERS

ADAMSVILLE

RHODE ISLAND
RED MONUMENT

77

NEWPORT

JAMESTOWN

SAKONNET

BEAVERTAIL
STATE PARK

Rhode Island Sound

NARRAGANSETT

1A

1

Ninigret
Pond

7

POINT JUDITH

WESTERLY

1

6

1A

MISQUAMICUT

NINIGRET
CONSERVATION AREA

Block Island Sound

WATCH
HILL

Block
Island

0   5   10   15

Scale

Facing page, top: *The fragile dune ecosystem at Watch Hill's Napatree Point is a haven for migratory birds and a favorite spot for birders.*

Facing page, bottom: *The Watch Hill Light station was established in 1806 by order of President Thomas Jefferson. The current granite tower, built in 1856, has weathered many storms well, though it did sustain damage during the great hurricane of 1938.*

Above: *Watch Hill emerged as an exclusive seaside resort at the start of the twentieth century, and the village retains an air of Victorian splendor thanks to the lavish beachside "cottages" built by elite summer visitors.*

Right: *Though not native to the Americas, Rugosa roses, also known as salt-spray or beach roses, thrive in shoreline habitats such as that of Rhode Island's Ninigret Conservation Area.*

Two young women ride sidesaddle on the Watch Hill Flying Horses in the early 1950s. The carousel was designated a National Historic Landmark in 1987. (Photograph courtesy of the Rhode Island State Archives, Acc. 1996-14, Economic Development Corporation)

the patient ones, though, as Watch Hill claims the oldest surviving Flying Horse Carousel in the United States. The hollow horses are each carved from a single piece of wood and outfitted with horsehair tails and manes, leather saddles, and agate eyes. They are suspended on chains and appear to soar as the merry-go-round gathers speed, and the children riding them—sorry, parents, but riders must be under twelve years old—reach out to grasp for lucky brass rings.

The carousel, built by the Charles W. F. Dare Company of New York in the mid 1860s, was unceremoniously abandoned in Watch Hill by a traveling gypsy carnival in 1879. It survived the great hurricane of 1938, which was not as kind to the Victorian cottages and grand hotels that were built during the seaside resort's heyday in the early twentieth century. Still, enough vintage buildings survive to imbue Watch Hill with the aura of times gone by. The public beach in Watch Hill, located behind the carousel, is tiny, but admission to it also includes views of Watch Hill Light. The 1856 granite beacon replaced an earlier wooden lighthouse from 1808. Unfortunately, the lighthouse could not forewarn the residents of Napatree Point that the 1938 hurricane was about to sweep their homes into the sea. A hike out to the point, now a conservation area, is a mile-and-a-half journey to one of New England's few true ghost towns.

Misquamicut, the next major beach as you motor eastward along the shore, may seem like a ghost town in the off-season, but when the heat is

WILD R.I.

For a small state, Rhode Island has a surprisingly large number of wildlife refuges, designed to provide protected habitats for finned, furry, and feathered natives and migratory visitors. Five National Wildlife Refuges fall under the jurisdiction of the U.S. Fish and Wildlife Service and are open to the public daily from dusk until dawn.

Along Rhode Island's South County coast, 400-acre Ninigret Refuge in Charlestown and 640-acre Trustom Pond Refuge in South Kingstown offer diverse wetland habitats for marine life, fresh- and saltwater pond dwellers, and an impressive variety of birds. The John H. Chafee Refuge, located on the Narrow River in Narragansett and South Kingstown, is a tidal salt marsh that provides an important migratory and wintering habitat for black ducks. It is primarily accessible via canoe or small boat, and views of the refuge can be had from Narragansett's Sprague Bridge and Middlebridge. On the other side of Narragansett Bay, in Middletown, Sachuest Point

Refuge provides observation platforms that allow visitors to view marshes, sand dunes, and rocky coastal areas that harbor abundant wildlife, including more than two hundred bird species. A short drive from Newport, the refuge is known for its saltwater fishing and for the East Coast's largest winter population of harlequin ducks. National protection is also granted to several sites on Block Island due to their importance as habitats for shorebirds, migratory songbirds, and several species of mammals and amphibians found exclusively on the island.

The Audubon Society of Rhode Island administers an additional 9,000 acres of refuge land throughout the state. Most are open to the public and offer maintained trail systems. The Emilie Ruecker Wildlife Refuge in Tiverton is a particularly picturesque location for observing and photographing great egrets, snowy egrets, glossy ibis, and osprey in a coastal marsh environment.

on, Rhode Island's longest state beach is rollicking. In addition to its 7 miles of sand, Misquamicut offers a multitude of amusements, including go-cart tracks, jet-ski rentals, kiddy rides, and miniature golf courses, as well as an array of souvenir shops and fried-seafood stands. Here, the collision of surf and turf has spawned a playland complete with tightly packed beach houses, resorts, family motels, and RV lots.

If Misquamicut sounds a bit wild for your tastes, you might prefer a wilder beach. Within the Ninigret Conservation Area, a 3-mile beach known as East Beach is preserved in a relatively natural and undisturbed state. The secluded barrier beach flanked by tall, billowy grasses and fuchsia beach roses separates a string of inland salt ponds from Block Island Sound. The largest, Ninigret Pond, is a popular windsurfing destination. Parking is limited, so crowds are as well, and while amenities are lacking, East Beach offers an opportunity to enjoy the shore's natural beauty, sounds, and scents. It's the perfect place to remind yourself that the ocean doesn't really smell like fried dough. If you own a four-wheel-drive vehicle, and you have planned ahead and obtained the required permit from the state's Coastal Resources Management Council, you can embark on a true backroads adventure—turning the dunes of the barrier beach into your own private highway.

FROM A LIGHT TO A LIGHT
THE SHORES OF NARRAGANSETT BAY

Watching wetsuit-clad surfers frolic in the foam off Point Judith, you might not realize that you are standing on a spot that nineteenth-century sailors called a "Graveyard of the Atlantic." The perilous point, on the west side of the entrance to Narragansett Bay, was the site of frequent shipwrecks due to the combination of rocky shoals and the same tumultuous waters that now make the bay New England's best place to catch a wave. As you begin this drive between two lighthouses, it's worth noting that these picturesque structures were designed first and foremost to save lives. The 1810 beacon that first warned mariners to steer clear of Point Judith was destroyed in 1815 when a hurricane known as "The Great Gale" hit Rhode Island. The present structure, built in 1857, is the third lighthouse on the site. Visitors can stroll the grounds surrounding the octagonal brownstone lighthouse, the bottom half of which is painted white, but you aren't allowed inside this active aid to navigation.

It's only a half-dozen miles from Point Judith to Narragansett—a beach resort area that competed with Newport during the latter half of the nineteenth century for the affections of society's most elite vacationers. The drive is lined with fishing areas, exclusive oceanfront homes, and beaches. Scarborough State Beach, a perennial favorite of Rhode Islanders, has 2,325 feet of ocean frontage, a boardwalk, picnic shelters, and an observation tower.

ROUTE 7

From the Point Judith Lighthouse, follow Route 1A/Ocean Road north toward Narragansett. At the Narragansett Town Beach, turn right to stay on 1A North/Boston Neck Road. After Casey Farm in Saunderstown, watch for a left turn on Snuff Mill Road. Continue to a left onto Gilbert Stuart Road and the Gilbert Stuart Birthplace. Reverse back to 1A, turn left, and head north to Route 138. Go east on 138 and cross the Jamestown Bridge. Take the right-hand exit for Jamestown and follow Conanicus Avenue south to Jamestown center. Conanicus Avenue becomes Walcott Avenue. Turn right on Hamilton Avenue, then left on Beavertail Road to Beavertail State Park.

Above: *The price tag for a home situated on Narragansett's bedrock shore may be steep, but the ocean's daily surf-spray show is thrown in free.*

Right: *Saunderstown's Community Supported Agriculture program entitles local shareholders to fresh, organically grown vegetables, fruits, herbs, and pick-your-own flowers throughout the growing season, while helping to sustain historic Casey Farm.*

Left: *Sailboats, many likely launched from Newport, can frequently be sighted from Beavertail State Park at the southern tip of Conanicut Island.*

You'll know you have arrived in Narragansett when you drive underneath "The Towers," a fortress-like granite structure that is all that survives of the famous Narragansett Pier Casino designed by the Gilded Age architectural firm of McKim, Mead & White and landscaped by Frederick Law Olmsted. Built between 1883 and 1886 during Narragansett's glory days, "The Pier" was the hub of social activity with its restaurants, shops, theater, ballroom, bandstand, and facilities for billiards, cards, tennis, bowling, shooting, and other sports. The grand casino was reduced to rubble when fire broke out on September 12, 1900. The Towers also survived a second fire in 1965, which destroyed McKim, Mead & White's 1905 replacement casino. The "indestructible" Towers now house a banquet hall and the Narragansett Chamber of Commerce's visitor information center.

Grand hotels and swanky soirées may be a thing of the past, but Narragansett still has the crescent-shaped swath of sand that first put it on the map. Narragansett Town Beach attracts crowds of surfers, swimmers, and sunbathers each summer. The nearby South County Museum tells the story of the region's agricultural and maritime past. As you cross the Pettaquamscutt River and leave Narragansett behind, the region's rural character becomes apparent. Tour the farmyard and cemetery at the 300-acre Casey Farm, a prosperous eighteenth-century plantation that remains a working organic farm operated by Historic New England. Just up the road, a quick detour off Route 1A takes you to the Gilbert Stuart Birthplace and Museum, which honors the prolific Rhode Island painter. Never heard of Gilbert Stuart? Well, you've probably enjoyed his work nearly every day. His portrait of George Washington has adorned dollar bills for more than a century. The eighteenth-century, red, gambrel-roofed house and an adjacent restored 1662 gristmill are open for tours in season.

McKim, Mead & White's Narragansett Pier Casino became a centerpiece of Narragansett social life in the 1880s. This photo shows the Towers in about 1899, before fire ravaged the grand casino. (Photograph courtesy of the Library of Congress, Prints and Photographs Division, Detroit Publishing Company Collection)

Unlike most travelers, who continue east in a beeline for Newport, you will turn south after crossing the Jamestown Bridge and head for the tip of Conanicut Island. The island was inhabited by Native Americans as early as 3000 BC. In AD 1638, Conanicus, the Narragansett sachem for whom the island is named, agreed to allow English settlers to graze sheep on the island. A group of colonists purchased the island from the Indians in 1657, and in 1678, Conanicut Island was incorporated as the town of Jamestown.

While studying the island's shape on a map, you'll have to employ your imagination to understand the origins of its nickname—Beavertail. At the tip of the tail you'll discover Beavertail Light in Beavertail State Park. Like its counterpart on the western shore of the bay, where your day's journey began, this sentry has a long history of protecting sailors in the relentless sea swells. The spot's first wooden lighthouse, erected in 1749, was the third lighthouse in the American colonies. The tower was burned by British troops in 1779 and was left unrepaired until 1783, when the new Congress asserted authority over the young nation's dozen existing beacons. Visitors today see the stone tower that was built in 1856 to replace its aging predecessor. You can venture inside the assistant keeper's house, which is now a museum. Not satisfied with seeing two lighthouses in one day? Newport's Castle Hill Light is visible to the east.

INSIDE RHODE ISLAND
THE ARCADIA MANAGEMENT AREA

Because Rhode Island is nicknamed "The Ocean State" and has 400 miles of shoreline, you may be surprised to learn that nearly two-thirds of the state is forested. In fact, the state boasts more forestland today than it did two hundred years ago, when settlers cleared large expanses for farming. The state owns about 10 percent of the nearly 400,000 forested acres, and these woodland habitats are managed and preserved by the Department of Environmental Management's Division of Forest Environment. For travelers who venture "inside" Rhode Island, these areas provide an alluring alternative to beaches and boardwalks.

You'll need to contain your surprise to a mild utterance such as "Well, I'll be danged," though, when you venture into the largest state-owned forest, the Arcadia Management Area. The Division of Forest Environment is serious about maintaining the forest's pristine qualities, and the list of prohibited activities outlined in the official regulations includes "use of profane language." The list of activities you can freely enjoy within the park more than makes up for this restriction: canoeing, kayaking, boating, hiking, mountain biking, fishing, hunting, horseback riding, birding, swimming, picnicking, and some of Rhode Island's best scenic driving, particularly in the fall, when dense stands of deciduous trees perform their flamboyant annual routine.

ROUTE 8

From the Connecticut–Rhode Island border, follow Route 165 East to a right on Arcadia Road, heading south. At the first stop sign, turn left to continue on Arcadia Road. When the road ends, turn right at the stop sign onto Route 3. Turn right on Route 138, which comes up quickly, and follow it west to the Connecticut border.

Facing page: *The water lilies that camouflage Browning Mill Pond are every bit as lovely—and much more fragrant—as any captured on canvas by Claude Monet.*

Above: *Residents of Sakonnet value their privacy and the peaceful character of this often overlooked corner of Rhode Island.*

Left: *Fishing charters and private fishing boats fill the harbor at out-of-the-way Sakonnet Point.*

As you enter Rhode Island on Route 165, the road bisects Beach Pond, which has a small swimming beach and a bass population that lures anglers. Route 165 also divides the Arcadia Management Area into north and south sections, each veined with trails, rivers, and brooks, all pulsing with outdoor enthusiasts hiking, canoeing, or wading waist-deep, waiting for the catch of the day—likely trout.

Remnants of stone walls along Arcadia Road hint at the agricultural chapter of the region's history, when seventeenth-century settlers wrested these lands from the indigenous Narragansett Indians by force or by finance. Beginning in the mid eighteenth century, farmers largely abandoned the area for more fertile tracts to the west, so the wilderness has had ample time to reassert its own, very valid claim.

If you've packed a picnic, stop at the Browning Mill Pond Recreation Area and dine alfresco overlooking a babbling brook, a cascading waterfall, or a still pond. If you plan to explore the forest on foot or by bike, or if you're licensed and ready to fish, this is also a good starting point for a day of adventure.

Arcadia Road turns left at the intersection with Summit Road near the Arcadia Warmwater Trout Hatchery, where many of the area's brook, brown, and rainbow trout got their start. Stop at the Division of Forest Environment's Arcadia headquarters at 260 Arcadia Road for a trail map and information on camping within the state-managed area. Once you've had your fill of this wilderness treasure, meander back to the Connecticut border on Route 138, passing ponds, farms, family campgrounds, and residential areas. You're outside the Arcadia Management Area now, so it's probably safe to resume your cussing.

GET TO THE POINT
THE SECRETIVE SOUTHEASTERN CORNER

Rhode Island doesn't end at Newport, but few tourists find their way east of the Ocean State's glittery city to the secluded peninsula that dangles into Rhode Island Sound. This often-overlooked Rhode Island outpost, separated from neighboring Aquidneck Island by the Sakonnet River, attracted its first European settlers from Plymouth Colony and was part of Massachusetts until 1746. Before the town of Little Compton was incorporated in 1682, the coastal area was known as Sakonnet, named for the native Sogkonnite tribe.

The southern tip of the peninsula—still called Sakonnet Point—is the objective of this drive. When you start out from Tiverton Four Corners, you will need to assess your aptitude for adventure. If you're a joy tripper, Sakonnet Point is a straight shot down Route 77 South. To catch a few additional sights and some very pretty countryside along the way, however, you can take a more circuitous route to the point, first heading east to Adamsville. Be forewarned: You may need to follow your nose, the

ROUTE 9

From Tiverton Four Corners, follow Route 179 East to Adamsville; stay to the right on 179 East when the road forks. At Gray's Store in the village of Adamsville, reverse direction on Route 179 and take the second left, onto Cold Brook Road. Turn left on John Dyer Road—watch for a handmade street sign near the cemetery. At the first stop sign, bear right on Pottersville Road. At the next stop sign, turn left on Snell Road (may be unmarked). When the road bears to the right, continue straight onto East Main Road, which becomes Maple Avenue, then Brownell Road, and then Swamp Road. When the road ends, turn left on Route 77 South and proceed to Sakonnet Point. Reverse on Route 77, heading north to Tiverton Four Corners.

sun, a compass, or sheer instinct as you navigate the local roads that meander southwest from Adamsville to Sakonnet Point. Many of the streets are unmarked—rumor has it that this is an intentional local strategy for thwarting tourists.

Tiverton Four Corners is the crossroads of this small and sparsely populated segment of Rhode Island. The town has a bustling village center with shops, galleries, and enough history to land it on the National Register of Historic Places. During the Revolutionary War, Tiverton Four Corners was a refuge and mustering point for American forces intent on reclaiming Aquidneck Island from British occupation.

Route 179 heads east from the village through residential areas and past small horse and livestock farms. After the fork in the road, keep your eyes open for the Rhode Island Red Monument, which commemorates the chicken breed that originated in Adamsville and later became the Rhode Island state bird. If you arrive at Gray's Store without seeing it, you won't be the first person to wander inside to inquire about it, only to be greeted with a teasing, "Did you think it was a big chicken?" Gray's, established in 1788, is one of the oldest continuously operating general stores in the country. Poke around and purchase some penny candy—just in case you get lost en route to Sakonnet Point—before reversing direction on Route 179. The first left turn is Westport Harbor Road, and it is at this corner that you'll discover the granite tablet with an embossed rooster image, dedicated in 1925 by the Rhode Island Red Club of America. An inscription states, "Red fowls were bred extensively by the farmers of this district and later named Rhode Island Reds and brought into national prominence by the poultry fanciers."

The Rhode Island Red Hen, shown in exaggerated form on this postcard, was adopted as the official state bird in 1954. (Painting by Ken Haag, 1968)

As you follow the local roads in a southwesterly direction toward Sakonnet Point, don't panic if you begin to feel a bit lost; there are a few small businesses along the way where you can ask locals to point you in the right direction—and hopefully they will! Seriously, it's not easy to get completely befuddled in this little corner of Rhode Island, and you will eventually wind up near the point one way or another.

Hop out of the car at Sakonnet Point and walk along the rocky ledge for views of sailboats cavorting, fishermen filleting the day's catch, and warning beams emanating from the Sakonnet Point Light, located offshore in the Sakonnet River. The cast-iron sparkplug lighthouse was built in 1884 and relit in 1997 after forty-three years of retirement. It is not open to the public but is visible from the shore.

If your nerves are a bit frayed from the earlier drive, mellow out for a spell at Sakonnet Vineyards and Winery on Route 77 before returning to Tiverton Four Corners. Since 1975, this beautifully manicured estate vineyard has taken advantage of a climate similar to that of the wine-producing regions of northern France. Complimentary tastings and tours are offered year round, and a bottle of their Rhode Island Red is a fitting reward for not chickening out.

PART III

MASSACHUSETTS: LARGER THAN LIFE

Facing page: *At daybreak on a crisp autumn day, Monument Mountain in Great Barrington provides sweeping views of the Berkshires region. William Cullen Bryant immortalized this peak in his lyrical poem about a Mohican maiden who threw herself from its rugged cliffs because of her forbidden love for her cousin.*

Above: *Winter is a time of hushed respite on Cape Cod. Off-season visitors can get a feel for the area's charms without fighting the crowds.*

assachusetts occupies much more than its 7,840 square miles of New England geography. It inhabits the collective consciousness of every American. From Plymouth Rock to Bunker Hill to Walden Pond, the Bay State's legendary landmarks loom large in the mental annals of anyone who has opened an American history textbook. For many visitors, setting foot within Massachusetts's borders is akin to a homecoming.

Those who visit the state specifically for history will find it center stage as they walk Boston's Freedom Trail or converse with Pilgrim re-enactors at Plimoth Plantation. Venture off the typical tourist path, however, and you'll quickly realize that history subtly permeates every corner of Massachusetts.

Drive to Cape Cod's tip and stand on the doorstep of America, as the Pilgrims did weeks before they ever set eyes on Plymouth Rock. Navigate a pass first blazed by native traders and warriors, and appreciate the pre-Pilgrim epoch often overlooked in tales of the birth of a new nation. Marvel at the Yankee ingenuity that sparked a covered bridge craze. Gaze upon Mount Greylock's hulking shape—with the right squint, you might see the same great white sea mammal envisioned by Herman Melville. Focus on the faces of passersby in the bucolic yet sophisticated Berkshires and develop an artist's eye for humanity, just as Norman Rockwell did from his Stockbridge studio. Or trade your copy of *The Perfect Storm* for a seat at the bar inside the Crow's Nest in Gloucester, and gain renewed respect for those whose lives still depend on the unpredictable sea—four centuries after the Pilgrims' leap of faith across the Atlantic.

History is past but also present in Massachusetts, and around every bend a new lens awaits to bring the hazy images of childhood history lessons into crisp focus.

ROUTE 10

From Route 41 in Egremont, follow Mount Washington Road toward Mount Washington State Forest and Bash Bish Falls State Park. Turn right onto West Street, following signs to parking areas for the falls. Reverse back to Route 41 North, then make an immediate right onto Route 23 East toward Great Barrington, watching for signs to stay on 23 through several winding turns.

Turn left and follow Route 7 North through Great Barrington. North of Great Barrington, watch for a right turn at a light to stay on 7 North to Stockbridge.

BOTH SIDES OF THE BERKSHIRES
BASH BISH TO STOCKBRIDGE

In the mid nineteenth century, Hudson River School painter John Frederick Kensett adorned at least five canvases with images of Bash Bish Falls. In the 1960s, Norman Rockwell immortalized Stockbridge's Main Street with his illustration of the bustling town center at Christmastime. Both scenes have changed little since the time of the artists' renderings, and the two subjects are a testament to the enduring duality of the Berkshires, the hilly region of western Massachusetts that has sung its siren song to artists and sophisticated vacationers for generations.

This ramble through the southern Berkshires begins on the wild side, where narrow, twisting, tree-lined roads lead you into the heart of a forest preserve and its pulsing twin waterfalls. Bash Bish Falls State Park is tucked inside the 4,000-acre Mount Washington State Forest. The forest boasts 30 miles of hiking and mountain biking trails and a limited number of primitive campsites. The adjoining Mount Everett State Reservation to the east offers 1,100 additional wooded acres to explore.

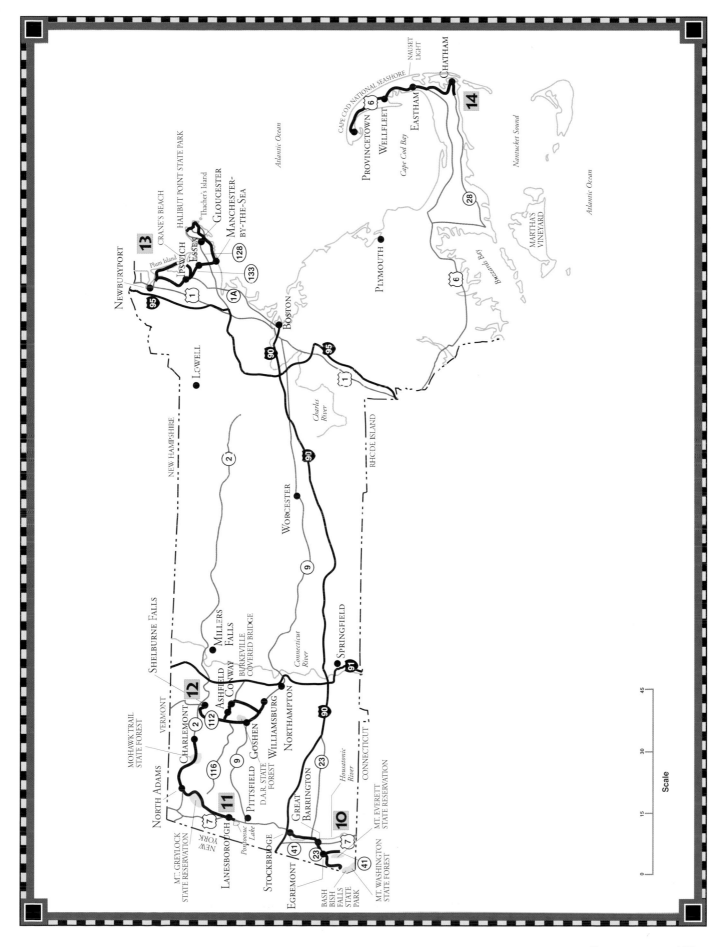

NAUSET LIGHT

CHATHAM

CAPE COD NATIONAL SEASHORE

PROVINCETOWN

WELLFLEET (6)

EASTHAM

14

(28)

Atlantic Ocean

Cape Cod Bay

Nantucket Sound

(6)

MARTHA'S VINEYARD

Atlantic Ocean

Buzzards Bay

PLYMOUTH

CRANE'S BEACH

HALIBUT POINT STATE PARK

Thacher's Island

13

GLOUCESTER

MANCHESTER-BY-THE-SEA

Plum Island

IPSWICH

ESSEX

(128)

(133)

NEWBURYPORT

(1)

(1A)

(95)

BOSTON

Atlantic Ocean

LOWELL

(90)

(95)

(1)

Charles River

NEW HAMPSHIRE

(2)

RHODE ISLAND

(90)

WORCESTER

(9)

SHELBURNE FALLS

MILLERS FALLS

ASHFIELD

CONWAY

BURKEVILLE COVERED BRIDGE

12

CHARLEMONT

(2)

(112)

WILLIAMSBURG

GOSHEN

NORTHAMPTON

Connecticut River

SPRINGFIELD

(91)

MOHAWK TRAIL STATE FOREST

VERMONT

NORTH ADAMS

(116)

(9)

PITTSFIELD STATE FOREST

D.A.R. STATE FOREST

(90)

(23)

Housatonic River

MT. GREYLOCK STATE RESERVATION

NEW YORK

(7)

11

LANESBOROUGH

Pontoosuc Lake

GREAT BARRINGTON

CONNECTICUT

STOCKBRIDGE

(41)

(23)

(7)

10

MT. EVERETT STATE RESERVATION

EGREMONT

(41)

BASH BISH FALLS STATE PARK

MT. WASHINGTON STATE FOREST

Scale

0   15   30   45

Spring brings apple blossoms, but summer is the season when Blueberry Hill Farm truly flourishes. Three varieties of highbush blueberries, the only crop that thrives in the acidic Mount Washington soil, have been cultivated here for more than sixty years.

Left: *The twin cascades of Bash Bish Falls, Massachusetts's highest waterfall, have been a popular Berkshires tourist attraction since the mid nineteenth century.*

Below, left: *In 1893, the town of Egremont appropriated $25 to establish the Egremont Free Library in the circa 1830 Egremont Academy building.*

Below, right: *Stockbridge's Red Lion Inn is charming year round, but there is something especially cozy about spending a winter evening in front of a warm crackling fire at this lodging and dining establishment.*

Many travelers skip the hiking and biking, though, and head straight for picturesque Bash Bish Falls. Driving in on East Street, you arrive first at the upper parking lot on the left, from which the waterfalls are a moderately strenuous, fifteen-minute hike; the second parking area on the left offers an easier walk to the falls. The pair of cascades, situated in an intimate woodland setting, forms a V as the waters plunge 80 feet over jagged boulders into a tranquil pool below.

As you leave the park and make your way toward the towns of Egremont and Great Barrington, enjoy the views of gently sloping mountain hills while counting the shades of green in the summer landscape or marveling at the panorama of autumn colors. In Egremont, you'll begin to glimpse the civilized side of the Berkshires. A clustering of antique shops, art galleries, and inns gives way once again to farmland strewn with horse barns and white clapboard farmhouses before you reach Great Barrington, where you leap from simply civilized to highly cultivated in a flash.

Speaking of flashes, would you believe that Great Barrington's Main Street was the first to be illuminated by alternating electrical current? Resident inventor William Stanley demonstrated the first AC system in 1886, lighting up twenty-four shops along the town's thoroughfare. Great Barrington also contributes to the Berkshires' cultural brilliance—it is home to the Aston Magna Festival, America's oldest summer concert series featuring classical music performed on period instruments.

Located just two hours from both Boston and Manhattan, the Berkshires have achieved a level of city sophistication uncharacteristic of such a bucolic enclave. In the mid to late 1800s, the region was "discovered" by wealthy urbanites, who built deluxe "cottages" and brought along their artistic sensibilities. Today, theater, music, dance, art, and history are prime draws for visitors.

Stockbridge is the hub of all that is happening in the southern Berkshires. Explore Chesterwood, the home and studio of sculptor Daniel Chester French, best known for crafting the seated Lincoln statue for Washington, D.C.'s Lincoln Memorial. Seek spiritual guidance at the

Norman Rockwell's Stockbridge Mainstreet at Christmas *depicts a classic Berkshires scene. Also known as* Home for Christmas, *the painting first appeared in* McCall's *in December 1967. (Photograph courtesy of the Norman Rockwell Art Collection Trust, The Norman Rockwell Museum at Stockbridge, Massachusetts. Printed by permission of the Norman Rockwell Family Agency.)*

Shrine of the Divine Mercy, a consecrated Catholic national shrine set amidst peaceful grounds that are open to all. Stroll flowered acres at the Berkshire Botanical Garden. Tour the Norman Rockwell Museum, which showcases many of the beloved artist's works, including all 322 of his *Saturday Evening Post* covers. You can also visit Rockwell's studio, which was moved to the museum site from its original location on Main Street near the Red Lion Inn; both structures are depicted in his famous *Stockbridge Main Street at Christmas*. The town's landmark inn opened as a stagecoach stop in 1773 and since then has operated continuously, with the exception of the year it took to rebuild the inn following a devastating fire in 1896. Dine, stay overnight, or sit on the porch if you can find a spot. The Red Lion Inn is the perfect place to pause and paint your own mental images of all that you have seen on this Berkshires drive.

NEW ENGLAND'S FIRST SCENIC DRIVE
MOUNT GREYLOCK AND THE MOHAWK TRAIL

Only in New England can a well-worn path retain its reputation as a "backroad." For centuries, the Berkshire region of northwest Massachusetts has been traversed by traders, warriors, and tourists. First blazed by five Native American tribes, the artery through this majestic mountain region has evolved from dusty footpath to paved highway, but the route—with all its scenic wonders—has remained essentially unchanged. On October 22, 1914, in the nascent days of America's love affair with the automobile, the 63-mile stretch of Route 2 from the Massachusetts–New York border to the Connecticut River was officially designated a scenic tourist route by the Massachusetts legislature. Known as the Mohawk Trail, New England's first official scenic road offers unparalleled natural beauty along with its assortment of country inns, gift shops, and arts attractions.

You don't have to drive over a mountain to get to the trail, but you really should if your travels take you to the Berkshires between mid May and mid October. From the smooth and meandering public road that leads 8 miles to the summit of Mount Greylock, views of the open valley expanses below will remind you of just how rural this part of the state remains nearly three centuries after the first European settlers arrived. Wind-bent birches furnish a canopy that dazzles in the fall and casts intricate and intriguing shadows on the narrow road whatever the season.

Herman Melville saw a great white whale in the snowy profile of the mountain and dedicated the book he wrote after *Moby Dick* to Mount Greylock. Henry David Thoreau and Nathaniel Hawthorne also found literary inspiration in the imposing form of this 3,491-foot spike in the western Massachusetts landscape. You're apt to be similarly impressed as you encounter Massachusetts's highest peak and the centerpiece of its first state park.

ROUTE 11

From Pontoosuc Lake, follow Route 7 North to a right on North Main Street in Lanesborough. Turn right on Rockwell Road and proceed to the summit of Mount Greylock. Drive down the mountain on Notch Road and continue north to Route 2 in North Adams. At the base of the mountain, make a sharp right by the Mount Williams Reservoir to stay on Notch Road. Turn right onto Route 2, the Mohawk Trail, and follow it east to a left on Route 8 North. Turn left on McCanley Road to Natural Bridge State Park. Reverse to Route 2 and continue east to the Mohawk Trail State Forest in Charlemont.

You may not find a pot of gold, but you will encounter emerald hills when you visit Mount Greylock State Reservation on a spring day.

The granite War Memorial Tower atop Mount Greylock was dedicated in 1933 to honor all Massachusetts residents whose lives have been claimed by war.

Located in Charlemont and known as "Hail to the Sunrise," this bronze statue of a Mohawk warrior embracing a new day is a monument to the Five Indian Nations that first blazed the Mohawk Trail.

Curvaceous and scenic Route 2 winds its way toward Florida—the Massachusetts town, not the state, as evidenced by the snow coat.

This 1921 panorama of the Mohawk Trail's Hairpin Turn shows the stunning landscape around North Adams. The peak of Mount Greylock is off in the distance on the left. (Photograph courtesy of the Library of Congress, Prints and Photographs Division)

When you arrive at the mountaintop, park the car and explore. The 92-foot-tall War Memorial Tower is an illuminated beacon that was originally intended to serve as a lighthouse on the Charles River in Boston. In season, the tower is open to the public, and those who climb to the top are rewarded with views of five states. The summit is also home to Bascom Lodge, a stone and wood retreat erected by the Civilian Conservation Corps in 1937. The lodge houses a snack bar, gift shop, restrooms, and rustic accommodations for thirty-two guests; reservations are a must. Hikers are common among the overnighters, as the famous Appalachian Trail passes through Mount Greylock State Reservation.

After descending Mount Greylock's northern slope, you will meet up with the Mohawk Trail in North Adams, historically the industrial and commercial hub of the Berkshires. The growth of North Adams's papermaking and textile enterprises in the 1800s fueled the need to widen and improve the road connecting the town with the Boston market. Today, the city's chief attraction is MASS MoCA, a 13-acre, 27-building former mill that was converted to house the region's largest museum of contemporary art.

For purists who want to start their Mohawk Trail trek at the very beginning, a jog west on Route 2 is an option. Lovely Williamstown is certainly worth a visit; the town is home to the Sterling & Francine Clark Art Institute and to Williams College, chartered in 1793 as the second college in Massachusetts and the sixth in New England.

Otherwise, continue east on the Mohawk Trail until you spot Route 8 North. You'll definitely want to see New England's only natural bridge. An abandoned marble quarry known for its rock formations, particularly the marble arch or "bridge" that was carved millennia ago by receding glaciers, became a Massachusetts state park in 1985.

Scenic overlooks present themselves at regular intervals on Route 2. You won't want to take your eyes from the road as you navigate the trail's notorious Hairpin Turn, but your travel mates will be awestruck by the far-reaching view of the Hoosac Valley, nestled among the Berkshire Hills.

Though the Mohawk Trail stretches another 27 miles to Millers Falls on the Connecticut River, you'll be ready to stretch your legs before then. The 6,457-acre Mohawk Trail State Forest in Charlemont is a good place to end your day's drive. Several original Indian trails within the park are open for hiking, so you'll have the opportunity, at last, to experience the Mohawk Trail as a true backroad.

FROZEN IN TIME
FRANKLIN COUNTY CONTRASTS

Franklin County, the most rural county in New England's most densely populated state, is a study in contrasts, and proof that the more things don't change, the more attractive they are. As you encounter the frozen-in-time towns of Franklin and Hampshire Counties, you may find yourself reaching for a map to ensure you haven't taken a wrong turn and inadvertently landed in Vermont.

Many Mohawk Trail travelers leave Route 2 to explore Shelburne Falls, but most return to the trail feeling that they have probably seen as much nostalgia as Massachusetts can offer. That's understandable, considering the village's attractions include a trolley museum, Victorian homes, shops where artisans demonstrate timeless crafts such as glass blowing, and the Glacial Potholes, a series of glacier-carved water holes at the base of Salmon Falls. Shelburne Falls' main attraction has remained the same since 1929; the one-of-a-kind Bridge of Flowers still delights those who stroll its

ROUTE 12

From the Bridge of Flowers in Shelburne Falls, follow Route 2A West/State Street toward Charlemont. Watch for a quick left uphill on North Street, and turn left at the end onto Route 112 South. Turn left on Route 116 South to Ashfield and, when the road curves to the left, stay on Route 116 to Conway. Turn right on Whately Road in Conway, and then right on unmarked Williamsburg Road, just past the reservoir and white chapel. At a fork in the road, continue straight on Nash Hill Road. When you reach a stop sign, turn left on North Street. Make a left onto Route 9 East to Williamsburg. Reverse and follow Route 9 West to Goshen and reconnect with Route 112. Follow Route 112 North to the D. A. R. State Forest and back to Shelburne Falls.

Colorful asters are among the more than five hundred varieties of flowers, vines, and shrubs that line Shelburne Falls' unique Bridge of Flowers, which blooms continuously from April through November thanks to the efforts of the Shelburne Falls Women's Club.

The Glacial Potholes at the base of Salmon Falls were created by the current-driven spinning of stones trapped in cracks in the bed of the Deerfield River. The potholes range in size from just inches to nearly 40 feet in diameter.

Left: *It's nearly impossible to venture inside the Williamsburg General Store without making a purchase, even if it's simply an ice cream cone.*

Below: *It's easy to leave the twenty-first century behind on a leaf-peeping drive through Franklin County towns such as Ashfield. The St. John's Episcopal Church has been a fixture here since 1829.*

expanse, whether they tiptoe among April's vivid tulips or amble among the orange and golden chrysanthemums of autumn.

If you take the time to venture south, though, you'll soon realize that Shelburne Falls was just a tease. If you've surveyed the surroundings, you may laugh aloud when you spot the "Thickly Settled" sign that greets you as you enter the town of Buckland on Route 112. Buckland's population is a few folks shy of two thousand. Of course, that *is* thick compared to the handful of settlers who arrived in 1724 and called their new home "No Town."

The towns of Ashfield and Conway may be diminutive, but they offer more than meets the eye. What meets the eye, mostly, are apple orchards, dairy farms, maple sugarhouses, and neatly planted rows of corn. The beautiful spire atop the Ashfield Town Hall will also attract your attention. The town hall was built in 1812, the same year that Ashfield's Samuel Ranney began growing peppermint and distilling peppermint essence. That simple act sparked a population surge, as the profitable business expanded to ten distilleries for peppermint, tansy, spearmint, hemlock, spruce, and wintergreen essences.

In South Ashfield, a detour on Williamsburg Road will take you to Chapelbrook. Chapel Ledge at nearby Pony Mountain is popular with climbers, and the series of three waterfalls at Chapel Falls is most impressive in the spring. Back on Route 116 South, keep your eyes peeled to the right side of the road for the Burkeville Covered Bridge, which spans the South River west of Conway center. The nineteenth-century bridge, also known as Conway Covered Bridge, is closed to traffic pending much-needed restoration.

From Conway, Whately Road leads to a partial-dirt road that provides the most direct access to Williamsburg. It also provides a scenic, if a bit bumpy, ride through what feels like an old-growth forest, although crumbled stone walls are your clue that this area was farmland at one time, too. A babbling brook runs beside the road, and ferns and wild outcroppings of mountain laurel thrive in the moist and shady environment. This glimpse of wild Massachusetts reclaiming its rights soon gives way to the suburban development on the outskirts of another classic Massachusetts small town.

Cheerful Williamsburg, with its stately Greek revival architecture and bustling general store, disguises the tragedy of its past. The one-time mill town was struck with disaster in 1874 when a poorly constructed reservoir burst, destroying mills, homes, and lives in its flood path. Today, the charming town is largely a bedroom community for the professionals employed by the five colleges in nearby Amherst and Northampton.

On your way back north through the Berkshire foothills toward Shelburne Falls, make a stop at the D. A. R. State Forest outside of Goshen for a final glimpse of untamed Massachusetts. In 1929, the Daughters of the American Revolution (D. A. R.) donated 1,020 forested acres to

THE CRADLE OF AMERICAN COVERED BRIDGES

Even though America's first roofed and sided bridge was constructed in Philadelphia circa 1805, one could classify Massachusetts as the cradle of American covered bridges. That's because the builder of that prototype bridge, Timothy Palmer, was a native of Newburyport, Massachusetts.

Why cover a bridge? To keep wooden trusses, a bridge's structural supports, dry and free from rot. Palmer and Theodore Burr of Torringford, Connecticut, were the first skilled craftsmen to make names for themselves building covered bridges. Though the concept originated in Europe, entrepreneurial New England carpenters transformed the covered bridge into an art form during the nineteenth century. Ithiel

Town of New Haven, Connecticut, Stephen Long of Hopkinton, New Hampshire, and William Howe of Spencer, Massachusetts, all developed and patented truss designs that were adopted by bridge builders throughout New England and across the nation. Howe and his associates came to dominate the industry. The 1870 Burkeville Covered Bridge, visible from Route 116 in Conway, Massachusetts, is a single-span variation on the Howe truss design.

Early builders believed that enclosing a bridge could prolong the span's life by forty years. We know now, of course, that many of these bridges have exceeded their expectations.

---

the Commonwealth of Massachusetts for conservation. The land, which has been augmented by an additional 750 acres, including Upper and Lower Highland Lakes, opened to the public as a park in 1936. Miles of trails provide opportunities for hiking, horseback riding, snowshoeing, snowmobiling, and cross-country skiing. A public access beach, campsites, picnic areas, and boat ramps for non-motorized craft are also available. In the fall especially, climb the fire tower on Moore Hill for sweeping views.

WHERE AMERICAN SEAFARING AND FRIED CLAMS WERE BORN
THE NORTH SHORE

Reminders of the riches that New England derives from the sea are pervasive along Massachusetts's rugged northern coast. Less frequent but more poignant are the reminders of what the sea has taken away. Any relationship with the tides is tempestuous, and man and land do not always prevail.

On a clear day, the line of sight from the 60-foot fire-control tower in Halibut Point State Park, at the northern tip of Cape Ann, stretches as far as the northern Maine coast. It is New England's only World War II tower open to the public. It was originally part of an elaborate system of several such stations that were integral to the defense of the ports of Boston and Portsmouth. The tower was situated near the edge of the Babson Farm granite quarry, which had ceased to be vital long before the Second World War. The sea wasn't the culprit in the quarry's demise; Cape Ann's granite

ROUTE 13

From Halibut Point State Park, turn left and follow Route 127 South to Route 127A South through Rockport. Turn right on Bass Avenue and then rejoin Route 127 South through Gloucester. Turn right on Lincoln Street in Manchester-by-the-Sea, following signs toward Route 128. Turn right onto Arbella Street, which becomes Pleasant Street, then right on School Street and cross Route 128. School Street becomes Southern Avenue. In Essex, turn right on Route 133 West, then right on Northgate Road in Ipswich, and another right on Argilla Road to the Crane Estate. Reverse back to Route 133 West and take that to Route 1A North. Turn right on Rolfe's Lane, right on Plum Island Turnpike/ Water Street, and left on Northern Boulevard to the northern tip of Plum Island.

If this red fishing shack in Rockport seems oddly familiar, it's because the structure, known as Motif No. 1, has long been a favorite subject of artists. Its image has adorned not only canvases but also countless puzzles, calendars, notecards, ceramic tiles, cross-stitch kits, and other souvenirs.

Rockport's Bearskin Neck, once the center of the town's shipbuilding industry, is now frequented for its quaint shops, art galleries, restaurants, and scenic views of Rockport Harbor.

Fishing is still Gloucester's lifeblood. While boats in port are a serene scene, at sea the risks are real: the U.S. Bureau of Labor Statistics identifies fishing as the nation's single deadliest occupation.

Winter weather and frigid seas make the job of fishing from Gloucester Harbor even more perilous.

industry went under in 1929 when the nation's economy plummeted into the Great Depression. A self-guided walking tour provides insight into quarry operations during the mid nineteenth through early twentieth centuries.

The village that flourished on this slab of granite was aptly named Rockport, and the demise of quarrying merely marked the beginning of a new chapter for this seaside outpost, which began to attract summer visitors and, in particular, artists. At Bearskin Neck Wharf, you'll discover restaurants, shops, galleries, and artists' studios in converted fishing lofts. The red fish shack beside the boat-dotted harbor may seem oddly familiar. Known as Motif No. 1, it has been the subject of countless paintings and photographs. When the shack collapsed during a fierce winter storm in 1978, a duplicate was built within a year.

From Eden Road, you can catch a glimpse of the Twin Lights of Thacher's Island, just over a half-mile offshore. If you're feeling adventurous, rent a kayak and paddle to the island. The Thacher Island Association also periodically offers boat trips, as well as opportunities to camp or to stay overnight inside the spartan keeper's quarters. In the seventeenth century, the Massachusetts General Court granted the island to Anthony Thacher and his wife, the only survivors of a 1635 shipwreck on the island. It must have been little consolation to the couple, who watched as the sea swept away twenty-one fellow passengers and crew members, including their children.

Route 127 is the main passage through Gloucester, America's first seaport, established by a group from Plymouth Colony just three years after the Pilgrims arrived in America. Most visitors come to Gloucester for whale watching, fishing, schooner excursions, ocean-view restaurants, and the gentle waves and expansive sand of Good Harbor Beach, but these pleasant diversions tell only half of the town's story. Gloucester still lives and dies by the sea, and it remains the North Shore's major fishing port. It has been home to Gorton's seafood company since 1849. The high school football team is known as the Fishermen. Life intertwined with the sea is rife with perils, and reminders of the ocean's power abound. Between 1830 and 1886, Gloucester lost 419 ships and 2,249 men on the stormy seas. As you sip a drink at the Crow's Nest, the local watering hole featured in Sebastian Junger's *The Perfect Storm*, you'll be reminded of the tragic true story of the men who perished in 1991 aboard the *Andrea Gail*. And as you approach the drawbridge at the west end of town, you'll see Gloucester's most recognized landmark, the Fishermen's Memorial commonly known as the "Man at the Wheel," a statue dedicated in 1923 to "They That Go Down to Sea in Ships."

Quiet Manchester-by-the-Sea boasts a cozy and picturesque harbor and the unique Singing Beach, where the white sand squeaks out a tune beneath your feet. If you're getting a little hungry, hasten on to Essex and Ipswich and embroil yourself in the great clam debate. You see, legend has it that Chubby Woodman invented the fried clam in 1916, and many will argue that the best deep fried whole bellies are to be had at Woodman's on Route 133 in Essex. Equally enticing, though, are the fried clams that have been on the menu at Ipswich's Clam Box since the restaurant opened in 1935. Try both and decide for yourself. Ipswich clams are renowned for their rich taste. Grown in the region's mud flats, they are less gritty than clams harvested from sand flats.

The Crane Estate is a worthy detour from Ipswich. Richard T. Crane Jr., who succeeded his father in 1914 as president of the Crane Company, a prosperous Chicago manufacturing firm, amassed a 3,500-acre seaside estate beginning in 1910. Today, 2,100 acres are the province of the Trustees of Reservations, a non-profit group charged with preserving the historically and ecologically rich property and making it accessible to the public. Play on Crane Beach, hike miles of trails through the dunes of Castle Neck, tour the Great House, or stay overnight at the historic guesthouse, now the Inn at Castle Hill.

Plum Island is a well-marked point of departure from Route 1A, so it's a little surprising that the 8-mile barrier island's beaches are relatively uncrowded, even when portions of this route are choked with summer traffic. Like all barrier islands, Plum Island is a gift of the sea, built up by tidal deposits. The southern three-quarters of Plum Island are part of the 4,662-acre Parker River National Wildlife Refuge. This favorite destination for birdwatchers offers trails and observation towers for viewing the migratory seabirds that frequent its salt marshes. Recreational shellfishing and surf fishing may be pursued from the refuge's tidal flats and beaches. The Newburyport Harbor Light, also known as Plum Island Light, stands on the grounds of the refuge headquarters at the northern tip of the island. The lighthouse's history begins in 1788, and it was none other than George Washington who appointed the light's first keeper in 1790. If you doubted the sea's potency, consider this: Damaging sea squalls and shifting sandbars have necessitated that the lighthouse be moved or rebuilt at least twenty-five times since it was first constructed.

Bessie Woodman, wife of the legendary clam man Lawrence "Chubby" Woodman, stands proudly outside Woodman's of Essex, where the fried clam was invented in 1916. (Photograph courtesy of Woodman's of Essex)

Above: *About 18,000 years ago, the last sheet of glacial ice slid northward to reveal an incomparable masterpiece—Cape Cod.*

Right: *Marconi Beach is one of six swimming beaches within the Cape Cod National Seashore's 40-mile stretch of protected oceanfront.*

Left: *In 1868, Captain Edward Penniman built his Eastham home in French Second Empire style. Visitors to the historic house, now a museum within the Cape Cod National Seashore, immediately know how Penniman financed this fine abode when they spy the massive whale bone arch in the yard.*

Below: *The Pilgrim Monument dominates the Provincetown skyline at dusk.*

ROUTE 14

Follow Route 28 South through Chatham and, at the rotary, continue straight onto Main Street. At a stop sign, turn right on Shore Road to Chatham Light. Reverse direction on Shore Road and continue straight onto Route 28. In Orleans, proceed onto Route 6A. At the rotary in Eastham, pick up Route 6 East toward Provincetown. At a light, turn right on Brackett Road, then left at the end on Nauset Road. Turn right on Cable Road, then left on Ocean View Drive to visit Nauset Light and the Three Sisters Lighthouses. Return to Route 6 East. In North Truro, turn left onto Route 6A to Provincetown. Turn left on Highland Road, then right on Lighthouse Road to Highland Light.

Anyone who has sat in traffic on the Bourne or Sagamore bridges, the only funnels onto Cape Cod, knows that calling any route through this narrow peninsula a "backroad" is a bit of a stretch. Still, even when summer swells the Cape's crowds, you can find pockets of isolation by outlasting drivers who ditch the road in Brewster or Hyannis and by pressing on to the Outer Cape. If you study the Cape's shape on a map, you'll see it resembles the pumped arm of Popeye after a case of spinach. The Outer Cape runs from Chatham at the "elbow" to the curved fist of Provincetown, where the Pilgrims first made landfall after sixty-five treacherous days at sea.

The voyage from Chatham to Provincetown isn't nearly as long or perilous; in fact, you could make the trip in just over an hour if you desired. Keep in mind, though, that the Pilgrims poked around for five weeks before relocating across Cape Cod Bay to the more hospitable environs of Plymouth—and that was before there were enticing shopping towns, seafood restaurants, lighthouses, and sandy beaches to visit.

Selecting a themed approach for your Outer Cape explorations can help to make a day's trip manageable. If ambling around in the consummate Cape Cod town is your objective, you'll be hard-pressed to choose between Chatham, Wellfleet, and P-town. As you follow Route 28 into Chatham, the weathered shingled homes, carved wooden porch sailors dressed in yellow slickers, and boats parked on lawns are a dead giveaway that you're on Cape Cod. Once you've found a parking place on Main Street, restaurants touting the local fleet's fresh catch compete for your attention with upscale shops filled to the gills with fashionable jewelry and clothing, collectibles, and imaginative Yankee creations. Wellfleet is famed for oysters and art galleries, and its cozy harbor is the ideal setting for nibbling fried shellfish. Provincetown offers great diversity in the shops and eateries huddled along its narrow streets, and salty air invigorates both the appetite and the compulsion to buy buoys that will look sadly out of place on your non–Cape Cod house.

Lighthouse lovers can breeze through the heart of Chatham to Shore Road, where Chatham Light guards the Cape's southeastern corner. The light station, now an active Coast Guard base, was established in 1808, and the current cast-iron beacon, which is not generally open to the public, was built in 1877. Off Route 6 in Eastham, four lighthouses are within walking distance of the parking area for Nauset Light, Cape Cod's signature lighthouse. The red and white Nauset Light, which hosts occasional open houses, was established in 1838, and the current 1877 tower was moved from Eastham to this location in 1923. A quarter-mile trail leads to the Three Sisters, a trio of lighthouses with a unique history. All were sold to private owners and removed from their coastal location in the early part of the twentieth century. In the latter half of the century, the National Park Service purchased and restored the lights, relocating them to a position not far from their original spot. Highland Light in North Truro, also known as Cape Cod Light, was the Cape's first, built in 1797 by order of George Washington. The current 1857 beacon is New England's brightest. For the ultimate lighthouse experience, Race Point Light in Provincetown accommodates overnight guests.

While boutique-hopping and lighthouse-spotting are fine pursuits, the Outer Cape's prime draw is its seashore. The 40 miles of beaches and wind-sculpted dunes from Chatham to Provincetown are encompassed within the 43,604-acre Cape Cod National Seashore; in 1961, it became the first seashore designated as a protected American treasure. At the Salt Pond Visitor Center on Route 6 in Eastham, you can get acquainted with the national seashore's array of beaches, hiking and biking trails, historic sites, and ranger-led programs. Even on busy summer weekends, the sheer magnitude of this sandbox makes it possible to find a secluded place to bask in the sun or amble along the grass-tufted dunes.

The Pilgrims wouldn't recognize Provincetown if they came ashore today. In 1620, the famous dunes at Race Point Beach were covered with a layer of soil and dense trees. Deforestation by early settlers allowed wind and water to effect monumental shifts in the underlying sand. Efforts to stabilize the dunes, which began in the 1800s, continue today through the National Park Service's beach grass planting efforts.

However you spend your day, a pilgrimage to Provincetown is not complete without a climb up 116 stairs and 60 ramps to the top of the 252-foot Pilgrim Monument. Catch your breath before the views from the top snatch it away again. Built in 1910, the tallest all-granite structure in the United States commemorates the Pilgrims' arrival on the cusp of this new, amazing, and ever-changing world.

This postcard map depicts many Cape Cod attractions (clockwise from upper left): Cape Cod Canal and Bridge at Sagamore; Barnstable sand dunes; Long Point Light, Provincetown; Pilgrim Memorial Monument, Provincetown; Highland Light, North Truro; an old Cape Cod mill; Wichere Harbor, Harwichport; a quaint Chatham scene; beach at Falmouth Heights; Nobska Light at Woods Hole; canal and bridge at Buzzards Bay; and a cranberry plantation.

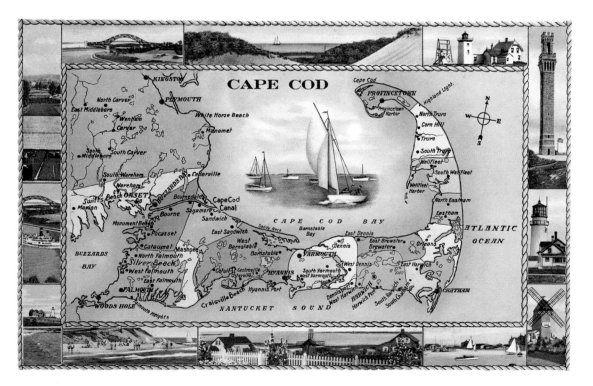

PART IV

VERMONT:
A PARADOX OF A PLACE

Facing page: *As the old song says, nothing is quite as romantic and hypnotic as "Moonlight in Vermont."*

Above: *Vermont is home to more than one hundred covered bridges, including the Henry Bridge in Bennington, which is actually a modern replica of an 1840 original.*

If you went in search of a place that defined the concept of "paradox," your quest just might lead to Vermont. New England's most agrarian state is also in many ways its most forward-thinking. Embracing such progressive ideas as agricultural cooperatives, socially responsible corporate policies, organic farming, and same-sex civil unions, Vermont has established itself as the region's rebel.

And yet, for those who buzz up Vermont's highways to schuss wintry slopes and even for those who take time to follow less-worn paths to the state's peaks and crannies, the overwhelming impression is of a place preserved, a stubborn holdout refusing to cave in to the pace of modern-day living. Here, white church spires still preside over tiny towns. Communities still gather on the green for village celebrations. More than one hundred covered bridges stand steadfastly over rivers and streams teeming with trout. More than two thousand maple syrup producers tap trees much as their Native American predecessors did.

With 4.6 million acres of unspoiled forests, more than three-quarters of the state is a vast timberland. And while dairy and other farms claim much of the leftover acreage, Vermont also has more golf courses per capita than any other state. Go figure.

Rather than trying to make sense of Vermont's contrasts, your time in this timeless enclave is better spent freeing your mind and embracing the contradictions. Vermont native Calvin Coolidge, the only U.S. president born on the Fourth of July, asserted in 1928, "If ever the spirit of liberty should vanish from the rest of the Union, it could be restored by the generous share held by the people in this brave little State of Vermont." A few days on Vermont's byways could go a long way toward resuscitating your own independent streak.

LOOKOUT POINTS AND UNDERCOVER BRIDGES
A STRUCTURED DRIVE THROUGH
SOUTHERN VERMONT

Manmade constructions are often considered blemishes in otherwise-alluring landscapes. Not so in New England. You'll find proof in abundance in southern Vermont, where historic structures add a nostalgic dimension to scenes or provide a means to a view you'd otherwise miss.

As you enter the state near Pownal, looming ridges shag-carpeted with leaf-bearing species provide a fitting welcome to the Green Mountain State; when autumn pounces, you might muse that Kaleidoscope Mountain State is a more apt moniker. A proliferation of apple orchards and roadside country stores touting local cheeses and maple syrup is another dead giveaway that you have arrived in Vermont.

The ultimate beauty of this corner of New England can be best appreciated when you're 306 feet, $4\frac{1}{2}$ inches above it all. That's a slight exaggeration, actually, as you can't access the tippy-top of the Bennington

ROUTE 15

From Pownal, follow Route 7 North to Route 9 West in Bennington. Turn right on Monument Avenue to Monument Circle and the Bennington Battle Monument. Reverse back to Route 7 and continue north to a left on Northside Drive, which becomes Route 67A. Turn left onto Silk Road to Silk Bridge. Return to Route 67A, and make a left onto Murphy Road. Cross Paper Mill Village Bridge and Henry Bridge, then turn right onto River Street. Turn left on Route 67A to Route 67 East. Turn left on Route 7A to Arlington, then right on East Arlington Road to the Chiselville Bridge. Return to Route 7A North, then turn left onto Route 313 West to the West Arlington Bridge. Return to Route 7A and continue north to Equinox Skyline Drive. Double back and continue north on Route 7A to Manchester.

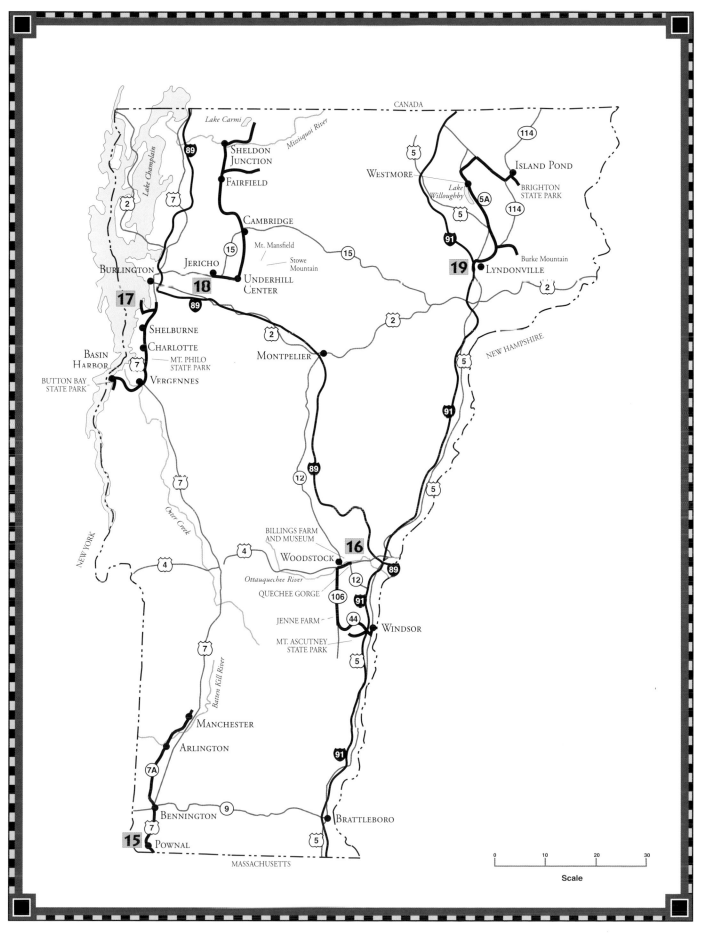

CANADA

Lake Carmi

Missisquoi River

89

SHELDON
JUNCTION

FAIRFIELD

114

5

WESTMORE

ISLAND POND

BRIGHTON
STATE PARK

2

Lake
Champlain

7

CAMBRIDGE

15

Mt. Mansfield

15

Lake
Willoughby

5A

114

Stowe
Mountain

91

BURLINGTON

JERICHO

18

UNDERHILL
CENTER

19

LYNDONVILLE

Burke Mountain

17

89

2

2

SHELBURNE

CHARLOTTE

MONTPELIER

NEW HAMPSHIRE

BASIN
HARBOR

MT. PHILO
STATE PARK

7

5

BUTTON BAY
STATE PARK

VERGENNES

91

7

Otter Creek

12

89

5

NEW YORK

4

BILLINGS FARM
AND MUSEUM

16

4

WOODSTOCK

5

Ottauquechee River

12

89

QUECHEE GORGE

106

91

7

Batten Kill River

JENNE FARM

44

WINDSOR

MT. ASCUTNEY
STATE PARK

5

91

MANCHESTER

ARLINGTON

7A

9

BENNINGTON

BRATTLEBORO

7

15

POWNAL

5

MASSACHUSETTS

Scale

0   10   20   30

Incomparable panoramas await those who drive to the summit of Mount Equinox on the longest privately owned, paved toll road in America.

Maple trees flank the approach road to the Bennington Battle Monument. The battle was fought on August 16, 1777, and Bennington Battle Day is a Vermont state holiday, though the Revolutionary War skirmish technically took place on New York soil.

The West Arlington Covered Bridge spans the Battenkill River, one of the Northeast's premier trout fishing streams. Nearby on the green is artist Norman Rockwell's former home, which is now a bed and breakfast.

Left: *Vermont-made products aren't limited to maple syrup and cheese.*

Below: *The Green Mountains' dense shades of jade are made possible by the efforts of each individual tree.*

Battle Monument, the monolithic limestone tower that dominates the Bennington skyline. In season, however, you can ascend to the observation level of Vermont's tallest structure for sweeping views that extend to neighboring New York and Massachusetts. The 1891 monument commemorates a Revolutionary War battle, which actually took place on New York soil, in defense of a military arsenal located at this spot. General John Stark must have been one of the nation's first great motivational speakers; his ragtag band of two thousand untrained volunteers from New Hampshire, Vermont, and Massachusetts rose to his bold pronouncement: "There are the Red Coats; they will be ours or tonight Molly Stark sleeps a widow." Molly got her hubby back, and the upstart Americans struck a decisive blow to the British campaign to sever New England from its colonial companions.

Two nearby landmarks provide additional diversions in this corner of Vermont. At Old First Church, you can hunt for the gravestone of beloved poet Robert Frost, which is inscribed with the epitaph: "I had a lover's quarrel with the world." (A hint—it's not an upright monument, so keep your eyes trained on the cemetery ground.) Next door, the Bennington Museum, established in 1875, counts among its treasures the largest public collection of works by Grandma Moses, the one-room schoolhouse where the late-blooming painter was educated, the lone remaining example of the only car ever commercially produced in Vermont, and one of the oldest surviving American flags.

The most pleasant route north from Bennington to Arlington takes quite a few twists, but it's worth it, particularly if you're traveling with someone you'd like to smooch. Covered bridges earned their reputation as kissing bridges back in the days of horse-and-buggy courtships, for they provided a blissful bit of privacy. Of the five bridges of Bennington County, the first you'll encounter, Silk Bridge, is the oldest, dating to 1840. On pastoral, farm-lined Murphy Road, you'll drive through two bridges, the 1889 Paper Mill Village Bridge and the bright red Henry Bridge, which was completely rebuilt in 1989. In Arlington, the 1870 Chiselville Bridge is posted with a warning that you'll be assessed a one-dollar fine for driving across the bridge "faster than a walk." Slow down as you cross the West Arlington Bridge, too, and enjoy your final make-out moments before returning to some serious driving.

Wipe the stars from your eyes before you navigate the hairpin turns of the Equinox Mountain Skyline Drive. This 5.2-mile toll road to the sky was built between 1941 and 1947 by Dr. Joseph George Davidson, who owned most of the mountain. The prolific chemist, who played a role in the development of the atomic bomb and rose to the position of president and chairman of Union Carbide, bequeathed the longest, privately owned, paved toll road in the United States to the Carthusians, a Roman Catholic monastic order, in 1969, along with nearly 7,000 surrounding acres. From the summit, the highest point in the Taconic Range at 3,848 feet above sea level, you'll be treated to incomparable views that encompass the Green, White, Adirondack, Berkshire, and Taconic mountain ranges and extend as far north as Montreal, Canada. Search the valley floor for the Battenkill River, which meanders through Manchester—your next and final destination.

The Battenkill is widely reputed to be one of the world's most challenging fly-fishing streams. Fittingly, Manchester is home to the Orvis Fly Fishing School and the American Museum of Fly Fishing. It's also home to a tourist-luring cluster of factory outlet shops, which, depending on your penchant for purchasing, may or may not detract from your appreciation of the historic 1761 village.

A SENSORY PATCHWORK
CLASSIC WINDSOR COUNTY

If you wanted to piece together a patchwork of classic Vermont scenes, you couldn't find better inspiration than a drive through Windsor County, a timeless landscape replete with covered bridges, vintage farms, mountain slopes, natural landmarks, and groomed greens at the nuclei of charming towns. This is a trip that requires as much parking as driving; frequent stops will allow you not only to view the sights between Quechee and Windsor but also to experience quintessential Vermont with all of your senses.

For example, you can see Quechee Gorge from high above as you cross over it on Route 4, but when you leave your vehicle and step out onto the pedestrian walkway or make the fifteen-minute hike to the bottom of the gorge, you can hear the tumult of the Ottauquechee River as it tumbles through this mile-long rocky swath. Seemingly cut with blunt pinking shears, the gorge is actually the product of glacial runoff more than ten thousand years ago. It may be a stretch to call this Vermont's Grand Canyon, but it's a worthwhile stop nonetheless, particularly when autumn leaves provide a colorful backdrop.

Roll down your windows as you cross the Ottauquechee River via the red-painted Taftsville Covered Bridge, one of the state's oldest covered bridges, dating to 1836. You'll then make an immediate left and follow a riverbank dirt road past farmhouses, stone walls, white-fenced paddocks, and an old cemetery. There's something about the sound of loose earth under your tires that adds a layer of authenticity to country driving.

The Billings Farm and Museum, at the end of River Road, is a preserved nineteenth-century working dairy farm and museum of rural Vermont. Across the street, you can tour the house and garden of the Marsh-Billings-Rockefeller National Historical Park. Admission to both sites can be purchased at the Billings Farm Visitor Center.

When you leave the farm, thread your way back to Route 4 West, which runs through the heart of Woodstock, the county seat for Windsor

ROUTE 16

From Quechee Gorge, follow Route 4 West to a right on Woodstock Road and cross the Taftsville Covered Bridge. Make an immediate left onto River Road, and when it ends, turn left on Route 12 South. Turn right on Route 4 West in Woodstock, then make a U-turn around the town green and an immediate right onto Route 106 South. In Reading, take a right on Jenne Road to Jenne Farm. Return to Route 106 and continue south to a left on Route 44 East. Turn right onto Route 44A South. Enter Mount Ascutney State Park and follow the Mountain Road to a parking area near the summit. Return to Route 44A South and pick up Route 5 North to Windsor. In Windsor, turn right on Bridge Street to the Windsor-Cornish Covered Bridge.

Above: *Few who drive along Route 4 through the village of Quechee can resist stopping to view Quechee Gorge, a narrow, jagged chasm carved by the Ottauquechee River.*

Right: *Hydrangeas flourish and the first hints of autumn dapple the hills behind Woodstock's Middle Bridge.*

A visit to the Billings Farm and Museum in Woodstock is a stroll back in time to Vermont's agrarian roots.

Housed in a historic armory, the American Precision Museum in Windsor explores the evolution of manufacturing and boasts the nation's largest collection of antique machine tools.

Frederick Billings began importing cows from the Isle of Jersey in 1871, and the Billings Farm and Museum is a working dairy farm to this day.

A sign at the entrance to the Windsor-Cornish Covered Bridge warned horsemen: "Walk Your Horses or Pay a Two Dollars Fine." The fine for driving an automobile faster than the posted 8-mile-per-hour speed limit was also two dollars. (Photograph courtesy of the New Hampshire Historical Society)

County since shortly after the town was founded in 1761. This quaint and historic town is a popular four-season destination thanks to its proximity to ski areas and family attractions. Woodstock Middle Bridge, on the northwest side of the village green, is a relatively modern covered bridge, built in 1969. Woodstock is also the only town in the world to claim five bells made at Paul Revere's Massachusetts foundry, and you can embark on a little scavenger hunt to find them all. Hint: One is located right behind the Woodstock Inn, on the opposite side of the green from the covered bridge.

A quick side trip in Reading will allow you to see Jenne Farm, widely considered Vermont's most photographed farm. It has appeared on magazine covers, in a Budweiser commercial, and in movies such as *Forrest Gump*. The farm is located on Jenne Road but is marked only by a tiny "maple syrup" sign. Indulge your taste buds and purchase a pint of the sweet stuff while you're there.

To treat your senses to the cool air and fabulous panoramas of a mountaintop, make your next stop Ascutney State Park, a few miles past the Ascutney Mountain ski area. From the entrance to the park, Mountain Road makes a steep ascent through tightly woven hardwoods to an elevation of 2,800 feet. Ascutney's summit is an additional hike of not quite a mile. The fire tower is an easier climb and affords views in all directions. On a clear day, you might see hang gliders taking off.

After descending the mountain, head for Windsor, the so-called birthplace of Vermont. It was here that the Vermont Constitution was adopted

In 1998, the Marsh-Billings-Rockefeller National Historical Park opened as Vermont's first national park and the only national park dedicated to the history of conservation and land stewardship in America. That story is embodied by three previous owners of the 550-acre tract of land, starting with George Perkins Marsh, who grew up on the property and went on to become a congressman, diplomat, and early environmentalist. His 1864 tome, *Man and Nature*, reflected on humanity's impact on the land and our responsibility to protect it.

Vermonter, lawyer, and conservationist Frederick Billings purchased the Marsh farm in 1869 with the goal of creating a model farm incorporating the ideas of land stewardship and forest management. Following his death, Billings's vision was sustained by his wife, his three daughters, and eventually, his granddaughter, Mary French Rockefeller, who, with her husband, Laurance S. Rockefeller, established the Billings Farm and Museum in 1983. In 1992, the couple deeded the remainder of their rural Vermont estate, including their Victorian mansion, to the National Park Service. Woodstock visitors can tour the Rockefellers' home and gardens for an in-depth lesson in the evolution of environmental preservation in the United States.

The Marsh-Billings-Rockefeller Mansion was a symbol of conservationist thought and practice before becoming the centerpiece of a national park. In this 1886 photo, Frederick Billings stands on the porch of the historic home. (Photograph courtesy of the Billings Family Archives)

Above: *Ascend Mount Philo for sweeping views of fertile Vermont valleys, island-dotted Lake Champlain, and the rugged silhouette of the Adirondack Mountains.*

Right: *Bright goldenrod sways in the breeze on this idyllic Vermont field.*

Left: *At Button Bay State Park, the limestone bedrock that borders Lake Champlain is the product of the fusion of ocean sediment, shells, and organic debris, a process that occurred about 450 million years ago.*

on July 8, 1777. Vermont was self-governing until it became the four-teenth state in 1791.

On Bridge Street in Windsor, you will encounter what may be the pièce de résistance for your Vermont image quilt. The 1866 Windsor-Cornish Covered Bridge is the nation's longest wooden bridge and the longest two-span covered bridge in the world. There's only one problem, which you'll discover when you reach the other side of the 460-foot lattice-truss expanse and see the sign welcoming you to another state. Owned by Vermont's neighbor to the east, the bridge is technically part of New Hampshire's patchwork.

VERMONT FOR SHORE
THE LAKE CHAMPLAIN VALLEY

ROUTE 17

From Shelburne Shipyard, follow Harbor Road to a left on Bay Road opposite the Shelburne Farms entrance. At the light, turn right on Route 7 South. In Charlotte, turn left on State Park Road to Mount Philo State Park. Reverse and continue south on Route 7. Turn right onto Route 22A and proceed through Vergennes and over Otter Creek to a right turn on Panton Road. Follow signs for Button Bay State Park, turning right on Basin Harbor Road. Turn right to continue on Basin Harbor Road to the Basin Harbor Club at the end. Reverse direction, continuing straight on Button Bay State Park Road to Button Bay State Park.

Don't pity Vermont for being the only landlocked New England state. Though it lacks ocean frontage, Vermont claims miles of freshwater coast along the shores of majestic Lake Champlain. Named for Samuel de Champlain, the Frenchman who first explored the lake in 1609, Champlain was designated the nation's sixth Great Lake in 1998. As you contemplate the placid waters from your starting point at Shelburne Shipyard, conjure up the wildest explanation you can for the origins of New England's largest lake. It probably won't compare with the tale handed down through oral tradition by the indigenous Abenaki Indians.

According to the Abenaki, a giant named Odzihozo gets credit for carving Vermont's landscape, including this spectacular 490-square-mile body of water. Because legs had not yet been invented in these early days, the legless Odzihozo dragged his hulking body about, gouging out rivers and valleys while piling up dirt with his hands to build mountains. He carved the vast lake into the valley between two towering mountain ranges and was so impressed with its beauty that he decided to retire from his earth-moving and turn himself into a rock in the midst of its waters. The spirit of Odzihozo is still believed to inhabit Rock Dunder, which juts up from the lake near Burlington.

With your imagination now inflamed, you'll also be able to envision how bustling Shelburne Shipyard was during its heyday at the dawn of the Age of Steam. The Lake Champlain Steamboat Company, later known as the Champlain Transportation Company, began operations here in 1820 and was responsible for the construction of a dozen sidewheel steamboats. The last steamboat, *Ticonderoga*, was launched in 1906; its home is now the Shelburne Museum, which you'll encounter shortly.

Odzihozo was certainly not the last to decide that the shores of Champlain, with its spectacular views of New York's Adirondack Mountains just 40 miles to the west, were a worthy permanent home. Harbor Road is lined with lushly landscaped estates tucked behind stone walls and tall lilac bushes that blossom with fragrant pink and purple flowers in the spring. This fertile valley also beckoned to Dr. William Seward Webb and Lila Vanderbilt Webb. In 1886, the wealthy couple enlisted Frederick Law Olmsted, the famed designer of New York City's Central Park, to help create their "model agricultural estate." Architect Robert H. Robertson was responsible for the Queen Anne–style manor house, which is now the Inn at Shelburne Farms. Today, the 1,400-acre property is one of the most beautiful working farms in America, and visitors can walk the property and participate in a variety of seasonal programs.

The town of Shelburne offers such varied attractions as the Vermont Teddy Bear Company factory and the Shelburne Museum. At the museum, you can explore thirty-seven historic structures, including a Lake Champlain lighthouse, a covered bridge, and a one-room schoolhouse, in addition to the steamboat *Ticonderoga*. You'll also get a peek at the museum's massive collection of Americana, which includes tools, quilts, carriages, circus memorabilia, paintings, and much more.

Once you reach Charlotte, commercial development gives way to farmland once again. At the Vermont Wildflower Farm, you can stroll among 6 acres of posies and other native flowers. For a bird's-eye view of the surrounding natural scenery, drive a narrow winding road or hike a steep trail to the top of Mount Philo. The summit provides scenic vistas and picnic facilities. Mount Philo State Park, established in 1924, was Vermont's first state park. The town of Charlotte is a departure point for ferries traveling to New York State across Lake Champlain. More than one million passengers cross Champlain via ferry each year, and this southern connection to Essex, New York, is just a twenty-minute trip.

Lake Champlain was once a vital shipping waterway for the Northeast. Here, the steamer Vermont *heads out from Burlington harbor, circa 1907, as the* Ticonderoga *passes in the distance. (Photograph courtesy of the Library of Congress, Prints and Photographs Division, Detroit Publishing Company Collection)*

Right: *In the late nineteenth century, Shelburne Farms was developed as a model agricultural estate on the shores of Champlain. Today, the National Historic Landmark remains a working farm, home to classic breeds such as these Jersey cows, and a testament to its designers' vision of a grand rural seat.*

Below: *Vermont is home to more than 1,400 dairy farms, and about 152,000 dairy cows live and work at farms such as this one in Cambridge.*

Above: *The seasons change, but the rigors of farm life remain constant. Vermont's hardworking farmers contribute more than a half-billion dollars to the state economy each year.*

Left: *You'll gain a new appreciation for snow after you view Wilson "Snowflake" Bentley's photographs of individual flakes, exhibited inside the Old Red Mill in Jericho.*

If riding the lake's waters is not of interest, you can learn all about the lake's storied past at the Lake Champlain Maritime Museum in Basin Harbor, which lies west of Vergennes. The maritime museum features a full-size replica of a 1776 gunboat and a working blacksmith shop, along with exhibits that tell the story of war, commerce, and recreation on the lake. At the end of Basin Harbor Road, the exclusive lakeside golf resort, the Basin Harbor Club, has been welcoming guests since 1886.

A less ritzy view of the lake can be had at Button Bay State Park. Situated on a bluff above Lake Champlain, these 253 acres of former farmland have been preserved for public enjoyment since 1964. Campsites overlook the lake, and there are boat rental facilities, a swimming pool, and a picnic area. A leisurely walk to the nature center at the end of the 1½-mile-long Champlain Foot Trail affords spectacular final views of the sparkling lake. Aren't you glad that legs were invented?

RURAL ROUTE
FOOTHILLS AND FARMLANDS OF NORTHERN VERMONT

ROUTE 18

From the Old Red Mill in Jericho, follow Route 15 East to a right onto River Road toward Underhill Center. At a stop sign, continue straight onto Pleasant Valley Road, heading north. At the fork in the road, turn left onto Lower Pleasant Valley Road. In Cambridge, make a right turn onto Route 15 North, then a quick left on Pumpkin Harbor Road (TH 2); TH 2 changes names several times as you continue northwest toward Fairfield. Approximately 1 mile north of Fairfield, turn right and follow a part-gravel road to the President Chester A. Arthur State Historic Site. Reverse to the main road and continue north to Sheldon. In Sheldon, take Main Street to a right onto Route 105 East. Turn left onto Route 236 North to Lake Carmi State Park.

If you've ever seen northern Vermont shrouded in snow, you probably never paused to contemplate the individual snowflakes stitched together in this blanket of white. Contemplating these frozen crystals, though, was what earned a self-educated Jericho farmer worldwide acclaim and the nickname "Snowflake" Bentley. In 1885, Wilson A. Bentley became the first person to photograph an individual snowflake. In his lifetime, he captured more than five thousand images of singular snow crystals using photomicrography—Bentley's pioneering technique of taking photos through a microscope. His work provided the basis for a postulate we now take for granted: no two snowflakes are alike.

A collection of Bentley's photographs is exhibited at the Old Red Mill in Jericho, where this drive through rural northern Vermont begins. The former Chittenden Mills, one of two mills remaining of the eight that once operated along Browns River in Jericho during the mid nineteenth century, also houses the Jericho Historical Society, a milling museum, an art gallery, and a craft shop, all open to the public. Study the snowflake images carefully. The appreciation you will gain for the mysterious individuality of nature's creations will serve you well as you embark on this drive, which may otherwise seem merely a journey past endless farmland and countless identical black-and-white cows.

You'll quickly spy the first of many herb farms, maple farms, dairy farms, and horse farms on the short drive from Jericho to Underhill Center. That is, if you can tear your gaze from the imposing, head-on view of Mount Mansfield, Vermont's tallest peak at 4,393 feet above sea level. With names like the Forehead, the Nose, and the Chin, the ridges along the mountain's 5-mile summit obviously suggest a human profile to many observers. Not visible from this vantage point are the ski trails of Stowe Mountain Resort that inhabit the mountain's eastern face.

Mount Mansfield remains in view for some time as you head north through some of the most picturesque agricultural acreage you're likely to encounter anywhere. Freshly painted red barns, oversized farmhouses, and wood-fenced horse paddocks belie the notion that farming is a fading pursuit. The University of Vermont's Proctor Maple Research Center, located on Pleasant Valley Road in Underhill Center, was established in 1946 as the nation's first facility dedicated to sugar maple tree research. The center is open to the public, and during the late February to early April sugaring season you can watch sap being transformed into syrup. Vermont is the largest producer of maple syrup in the United States, with an estimated $15 million in direct sales each year.

If you blink, you might miss some of the tiny towns along this route—some indistinguishable but for the presence of a general store—but larger towns would be amiss in this pastoral place. Here you're more likely to see a team of draft horses pulling a plow than a teenager flipping a burger. Just north of Fairfield, keep your eyes peeled for signs directing you to the reconstructed birthplace of Chester A. Arthur, one of two U.S. presidents to hail from the Green Mountain State.

When you turn east out of Sheldon Junction on Route 105, you will be treated to spectacular views of the mighty Missisquoi River on your right. Winding 74 miles through Vermont countryside before emptying into Lake Champlain, this river lures fly fishermen, canoeists, and kayakers. A recreation trail provides walking, hiking, and biking access along the river.

Cows and sprawling, well-maintained farms still dominate the landscape as you travel through Sheldon Junction and North Sheldon. The Canadian border is just a handful of miles away as you turn north toward Lake Carmi State Park, situated on the shores of Vermont's fourth-largest lake. The park is home to the state's largest campground; a beach and rental boats are available to both overnight and day-use visitors.

You always believed that no two snowflakes were alike, even before you saw photographic proof. After this drive, you also may believe the old saying that there are more cows than people in Vermont. But it's not true.

Wilson Bentley's microphotographs proved not only that no two snowflakes are alike, but also that they are stunning in their intricacy and symmetry. (Photograph courtesy of the Jericho Historical Society, "Snowflake" Bentley Collection)

Route 5A in Westmore hugs the shore of Lake Willoughby.

A proliferation of pumpkins is a surefire sign that it's autumn in Vermont. At Bailey's Country Store in East Burke, you can assemble the perfect fall picnic from their array of local specialty foods and their well-stocked wine cellar.

The sun casts a warm glow over Westmore's former one-room schoolhouse, but fall leaves hint at the chill that surely fills the air.

Above: *Mount Pisgah flanks the eastern shore of tranquil Lake Willoughby. Though summer is the lake's busy tourism time, high season in the Northeast Kingdom is still incredibly peaceful by New England standards.*

Left: *Mount Pisgah and Mount Hor are the only lifeguards, and the water is quite cool, but a dip in the crystalline liquid of Lake Willoughby is an otherworldly experience.*

A World Apart
The Northeast Kingdom

ROUTE 19

From I-91, take Exit 23 and follow Route 5 North through Lyndonville. Turn right onto Route 114 North, and take another right on Mountain Road. Proceed past the Burke Mountain Ski Area, and turn left onto the toll road that leads to the summit of Burke Mountain. Drive back down the mountain, turn right on Mountain Road, then left onto 114 South. Turn right onto Burke Hollow Road to West Burke, then right onto Route 5A North. Follow 5A along the shore of Lake Willoughby to Westmore and turn right on Hinton Hill Road by the Westmore Community Church. At the end of this partially unpaved road, turn right on Hudson Road. Turn right at the end of Hudson Road and follow Route 105 East to Island Pond. Take a right on Pleasant Street, followed by a left on Lake Shore Drive to Brighton State Park.

With the onset of the American Revolution, New York and New Hampshire put aside their squabbles over the territory betwixt them in order to confront a common enemy—the British. Settlers in the disputed territory saw an opening, and on January 15, 1777, they formed the free and independent republic of New Connecticut. When the Continental Congress of the fledgling United States rejected this claim of sovereignty, the citizens of New Connecticut stubbornly charged forward, drafting their own constitution and renaming their country the Independent Republic of Vermont. For fourteen years, Vermont minted its own money, operated its own postal system, made its own laws, and conducted trade with foreign countries—including the United States.

When you visit Vermont's far northeastern corner today, you may wonder if these parts ever got word that the republic joined the union in 1791. Covering three counties and 2,000 square miles, this wild and sparsely populated region remains a world apart. In 1949, U.S. Senator George Aiken of Vermont christened it the "Northeast Kingdom."

If Lyndonville, Vermont, sounds familiar, it probably means that at one time or another you've purchased a distinctive green tin can of Bag Balm. Originally designed to soothe chapped cow udders, this balm is now sold widely in drugstores to offer the same skin-healing properties to humans. The softening salve has been made in Lyndonville for more than one hundred years.

Before you leave Lyndonville, fill the car up with gas, and be sure to ask for change in singles. The Northeast Kingdom's idea of a toll road is a bit different than what you may be accustomed to if you hail from, say, New Jersey. At the toll road that leads to the summit of Burke Mountain, you may be greeted by a simple sign that reads: "Put money in box. $3 cars - $2 seniors - $1 motorcycles."

You're in for an ear-popping ride as you navigate the tight turns leading 3,267 feet to the mountaintop. The toll road is open from mid May to mid October during daylight hours. When you park at the peak and emerge from your car, breathe deeply. For a second, you might imagine that you're in a warehouse filled with tree-shaped car fresheners—the scent of pine is that overpowering. A five-story observation tower affords far-reaching views of New Hampshire's White Mountains to the east and Lake Willoughby to the north, even if you climb only as high as the first platform.

The distinctive land formations of this realm were chiseled as the last batch of Ice Age glaciers receded some twelve thousand years ago. Narrow, 5-mile Lake Willoughby, the region's deepest lake, is perhaps the glaciers' greatest bequest. Standing on the natural sand beach at the south end of the lake, you will be amazed at how far out from shore the lake bottom remains visible and how magically the crystalline waters reflect the twin cliffs of Mount Pisgah to the east and Mount Hor to the west. Lake Willoughby is nicknamed the Lucerne of America, but unlike its Swiss namesake, this watery gem is not overrun with tourists. Those who flock to the lake to fish, hike, boat, and bike enjoy relative peacefulness even during peak season, and those adventurers who know this as an awesome site for winter ice climbing have few spectators for their daring exploits.

As you head east from Westmore, don't forget to check your rearview mirror for a few last spectacular glimpses of the lake's blue hues and the seasonal colorations of the forested mountains. If weather conditions make the drive east on partially dirt roads potentially treacherous, you might opt to continue north on Route 5A to Route 105 East, which will take you to the Village of Island Pond in the town of Brighton.

Island Pond's place in history comes from being the home of the first international railroad junction in the United States. From the 1850s until the Great Depression, Island Pond thrived as the halfway station between Montreal and Boston on the Grand Trunk Railroad line. Today, only two of the original thirteen tracks remain in operation, but an exhibit inside the old train station tells the story of the village's heyday. They may no longer arrive by rail, but folks do still find their way to nearby Brighton State Park, situated between Island Pond and Spectacle Pond. This preserved wilderness area offers camping, picnicking, hiking, swimming, birding, fishing, and cross-country skiing.

A drive through the Northeast Kingdom requires a day, a tank of gas, a roll or two of film, and the pioneering spirit to take on what has been called New England's final frontier. Luckily, it doesn't require a passport.

PART V

NEW HAMPSHIRE:
LIVE FREE OR DIE

Facing page: *The mill pond on Route 10 in Marlow reflects a classic New England scene, neatly framed by spindly birch trees.*

Above: *In summer, only a camera can hold the rush of Beaver Brook Falls, but in winter, this Great North Woods cascade is often literally frozen in time.*

You could meander through any other New England state and depart without knowing its official motto, but that's practically impossible in New Hampshire, where "Live Free Or Die" is emblazoned on license plates, signs, and souvenirs. What is the origin of this bold phrase?

The four-word maxim was penned by New Hampshire's most famous Revolutionary War veteran and hero of the 1777 Battle of Bennington, General John Stark. It was thirty-two years after that pivotal battle, and the veterans were planning a reunion. In begging off due to ill health, Stark sent this toast to his former comrades: "Live Free Or Die; Death Is Not The Worst Of Evils."

Though America's war for independence is far removed from the consciousness of most New Hampshire travelers, the phrase "Live Free or Die" still resonates. It is a call to live life to the utmost, to roam freely, to absorb the wonders of nature, and to revel in the infinite variety of living things. New Hampshire's geographic diversity provides unlimited back-drops against which to stage a personal escape from the shackles of the workaday world. Hide away in the dense tangle of the Great North Woods where moose make the rules. Visualize the future from the uninterrupted sightline of a snow-capped mountaintop. Ponder the ripple patterns on lakes and ponds. Add your beach umbrella to the sea of humanity on New England's shortest shoreline, or wait until the days grow shorter and the crowds thinner, and claim the ocean as your own.

There is no wrong way to experience the Granite State, but to miss New Hampshire—that might be the worst of evils.

ELEPHANTS, DONKEYS, AND MOOSE
THE GREAT NORTH WOODS

ROUTE 20

From Errol, follow Route 26 West through Dixville Notch to Colebrook, turn right on Route 3 North, then a quick right onto Route 145 North to Pittsburg. In Pittsburg, turn left onto Route 3 South and make a left on Fletcher Road to the Pittsburg-Clarksville Covered Bridge. Return to Route 3 and head north. Approximately 6 miles north of Pittsburg Village, turn right on Hill Road to the Happy Corner Covered Bridge. Return to Route 3 and continue north to the Canadian border.

The Great North Woods is home to the majority of New Hampshire's nearly ten thousand moose. In fact, the stretch of Route 3 from Pittsburg, the state's northernmost town, to the Canadian border is known as "Moose Alley." Highway signs warn: "Brake for Moose. It Could Save Your Life. Hundreds of Collisions." Every four years, though, the moose must share the spotlight with another breed—political animals.

Every elected U.S. president since Dwight D. Eisenhower has followed the campaign trail to Dixville Notch, New Hampshire. Why? To woo the thirty-some-odd voters of this remote township. Since 1960, the citizens of Dixville Notch have had the honor of being the first to weigh in when New Hampshire holds the nation's first primary each presidential election season. At midnight on election day, the entire populace of Dixville Notch convenes inside the Ballot Room at The Balsams Grand Resort Hotel to cast its votes. The polls are then promptly closed, and the results are broadcast across the country and around the globe by members of the media hungry for the first election results.

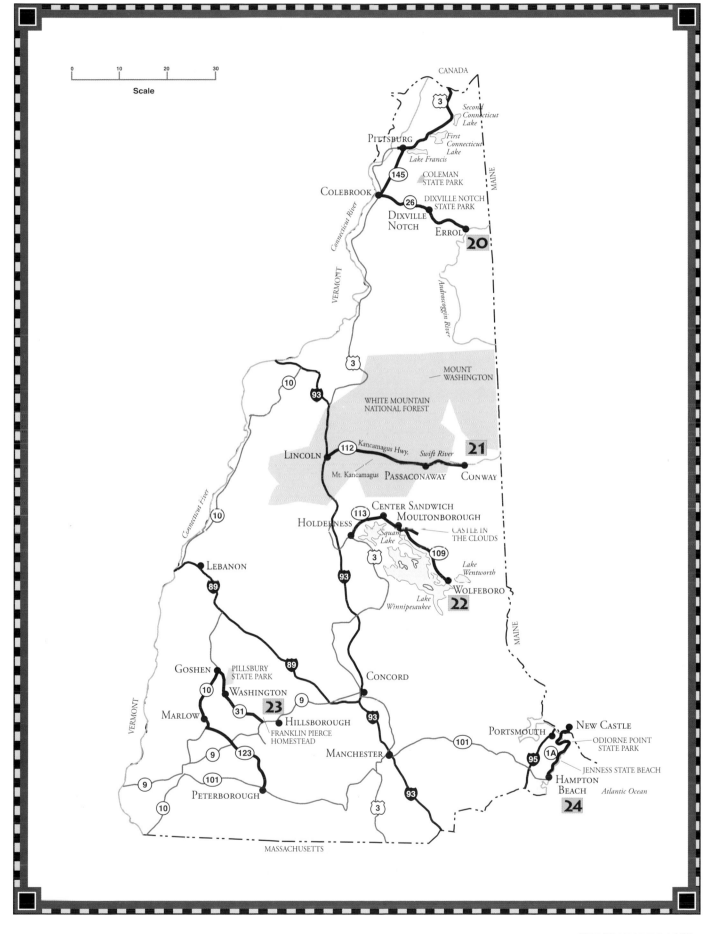

Scale

0   10   20   30

CANADA

3
Second Connecticut Lake

First Connecticut Lake

PITTSBURG

Lake Francis

145

COLEMAN STATE PARK

COLEBROOK

26
DIXVILLE NOTCH STATE PARK

DIXVILLE NOTCH

ERROL

20

VERMONT

MAINE

Androscoggin River

Connecticut River

3

MOUNT WASHINGTON

10

93

WHITE MOUNTAIN NATIONAL FOREST

LINCOLN

112

Kancamagus Hwy.

Swift River

21

Mt. Kancamagus

PASSACONAWAY

CONWAY

10

CENTER SANDWICH

MOULTONBOROUGH

113

HOLDERNESS

Squam Lake

CASTLE IN THE CLOUDS

3

109

Lake Wentworth

93

WOLFEBORO

22

LEBANON

89

Lake Winnipesaukee

Connecticut River

MAINE

89

GOSHEN

PILLSBURY STATE PARK

CONCORD

10

WASHINGTON

9

93

MARLOW

31

23

HILLSBOROUGH

FRANKLIN PIERCE HOMESTEAD

101

PORTSMOUTH

NEW CASTLE

ODIORNE POINT STATE PARK

95

1A

9

123

MANCHESTER

93

JENNESS STATE BEACH

VERMONT

9

101

HAMPTON BEACH

24

10

PETERBOROUGH

Atlantic Ocean

3

93

MASSACHUSETTS

Pittsburg, New Hampshire's largest town by area, occupies 190,000 sparsely populated acres of the Great North Woods.

Above: *High in the White Mountains, steep and winding Route 26 cleaves closely to the towering, rocky cliffs of Dixville Notch. For more than 125 years, leisure seekers have traveled this route to a heavenly grand hotel—The Balsams.*

Left: *A bull or male moose's antlers begin as velvet-covered nubs in the spring, and over the course of just a few months, grow into an enormous rack that can weigh as much as 75 pounds.*

The Balsams in Dixville Notch was a popular New Hampshire resort long before it became the starting line for every presidential election race. (Photograph courtesy of the Library of Congress, Prints and Photographs Division, Detroit Publishing Company Collection)

Route 26 cuts a dramatic, 1½-mile slice through the steep, rocky cliffs of Dixville Notch State Park on its way to The Balsams resort. The grand estate claims 15,000 of the 31,000 acres in the unincorporated township of Dixville, making the resort larger than the island of Manhattan. The storied resort has welcomed guests since 1874, and the entire hotel, with its famed Ballot Room, is a showcase for political and cultural artifacts. Heavenly American Plan dining; one of New England's premier, Donald Ross–designed golf courses; alpine and cross-country ski areas; a trout-stocked lake; and night-club entertainment are but a few of the delights that await overnight visitors.

Don't be surprised, as you continue along toward Colebrook, if you don't recognize the music—or the language—on the few radio stations your tuner is able to retrieve. You're close enough to the Canadian border to pick up French-language broadcasts. A former lumber town founded in 1770, Colebrook today attracts outdoor enthusiasts and moose fans, who can sample moose stew and compete in a moose-calling contest during the town's annual summer Moose Festival. On the way to Colebrook from Dixville, you'll pass Coleman State Park, a haven for hikers, hunters, and fishing enthusiasts on the forested shores of Little Diamond Pond.

As you follow Route 145 North toward Pittsburg, stay alert not just for moose but also for Beaver Brook Falls, a photogenic cascade that comes up on the right without warning just a few miles north of Colebrook. The verdant knoll beside the falls is a perfect picnic spot, and, if you're adventurous, a plunge in the cold, pummeling water or even a twirl in the cool mist is a surefire way to awaken your senses. Also on Route 145, just before Clarksville Pond, keep your eyes peeled for an historical marker that informs you that you've reached the forty-fifth parallel—the halfway point between the equator and the North Pole.

Here in New Hampshire's outer limits, the seamless meeting of cloud-sprinkled sky and dappled mountain ridges may cause you to wonder whether the scene before you isn't actually a Hollywood set. There are two covered bridges nearby that could be carefully crafted props. In reality, though, the Pittsburg-Clarksville Covered Bridge and Happy Corner Covered Bridge are monuments to New Englanders' nineteenth-century engineering prowess.

An outing on Mount Washington's "Road to the Sky" became an even more popular activity with the advent of the motorcar. (Photograph courtesy of the New Hampshire Historical Society)

New England's highest point is the 6,288-foot summit of Mount Washington. And yes, you can drive there, just as folks have done ever since the 8-mile "Road to the Sky" opened in 1861. The Mount Washington Auto Road, accessible from Route 16 north of Pinkham Notch, is something of an engineering marvel, constructed before the invention of dynamite or motorized vehicles. It is now recognized as the nation's first manmade attraction.

The summit is above the tree line, allowing for unobstructed views of the Presidential Range and beyond. What was once a day-long outing by horse-drawn wagon is now a relatively comfortable, hour-long roundtrip drive. If you step outside your vehicle, be forewarned: Mount Washington didn't earn its reputation as home of the world's worst weather for nothing. Snow lingers here well after the arrival of summer, and since 1934, the mountaintop has held the record for the world's gustiest wind—231 miles per hour. If you need to escape the gusts, step inside the Mount Washington Observatory Museum, which presents exhibits on the natural history of Mount Washington and the Presidential Range.

The Auto Road is privately owned, and admission is charged. Dates of operation are weather-dependent, but it is usually open from early May until sometime in October. While most cars can make the ascent without a hitch, there are some restrictions on the types of vehicles permitted. Guided van tours are an available alternative.

In Colebrook, the summer landscape is saturated with color, from a sun-soaked field of golden dandelions to the cloud-woven cobalt sky above.

On First Connecticut Lake, the early fisherman catches the lake trout and salmon that are already searching for a snack at sunrise.

Above: *The Kancamagus Highway mimics the undulating course of the Swift River.*

Left: *Albany Covered Bridge, located on the north side of the Kanc at the Covered Bridge Camp ground exit, provides safe passage across the icy Swift River.*

The watery wonders along Route 3 will wow you with their beauty, and all are pristine and popular with paddlers. Lake Francis, First Connecticut Lake, Second Connecticut Lake, Third Connecticut Lake, and Fourth Connecticut Lake form the headwaters of the 400-mile-long Connecticut River, which bisects New England as it flows toward its Long Island Sound destiny. A public-private partnership is working to preserve 171,500 acres of this wetlands area. It serves as a habitat for a variety of animals and birds, including several rare species.

If you haven't already spotted a moose or two, don't despair. Moose Alley affords many opportunities to view these gangly creatures, which weigh an average of 1,200 pounds. Early morning and dusk are the best times for moose sightings. The residents of the Great North Woods may have a say in who will preside over the nation, but they know that moose rule the roads up here, so signs urging caution are abundant. Drive slowly, pull off the road completely, don't get too close, and keep your lens cap off.

THE FEARLESS ONE
THE KANCAMAGUS HIGHWAY

ROUTE 21

Follow Route 112, the Kancamagus Highway, west from Conway to Lincoln.

New Hampshire's National Scenic Byway with the tongue-twister name—the Kancamagus Highway—is New England's most superb scenic drive. You can call it "the Kanc" for short, as locals do, and you can revel in the pure pleasure of motoring through this thickly treed mountain gap, as more than a million visitors do each year. The 34-mile road cuts an east-west channel through the 800,000-acre White Mountain National Forest. When the dense stands of leafy deciduous trees exchange their summer greens for the dazzling shades of autumn, they are illuminated against the immutable evergreen of their coniferous counterparts, making this a most dramatic and beloved leaf-peeping route. Motorcyclists relish the twists and turns as the highway climbs to nearly 3,000 feet at the peak of Mount Kancamagus. Easily accessible trailheads summon hikers, and rocky swimming holes, carved by erosion, lure families craving relief from summer's swelter.

Though it maintains a legendary reputation among scenery seekers, the Kancamagus Highway is a relatively new route, as New England scenic byways go. Some old logging roads and town roads edged into the rugged National Forest, which was set aside for conservation by the federal government in 1911, but a connection between Conway and Lincoln was not completed until 1959. The road was paved in 1964, and in 1968 it was plowed for the first time, allowing for year-round traffic. New Hampshire State Route 112 is named for Chief Kancamagus, "The Fearless One." Kancamagus was the last leader of the Penacook Confederacy, a union of more than seventeen central New England Indian tribes, first forged by Kancamagus's grandfather, Passaconaway, in 1627. Kancamagus tried to maintain peace between his people and encroaching English settlers, but war and bloodshed forced the tribes to scatter, with most retreating to northern New Hampshire and Canada.

At the Saco Ranger Station just west of Conway, you can pick up a map and begin to plot your stops at the various well-designated scenic overlooks, campgrounds, picnic areas, hiking trails, and historic sites along the Kanc. Unless you plan to drive straight through without stopping, you'll also need to purchase a parking pass. A visitor information center is also located on the western end of the Kanc in Lincoln, should you decide to drive the route in reverse.

As you enter the White Mountain National Forest, you'll notice that the highway follows the path of the Swift River, which is studded with large boulders that create an obstacle course for the water. The river surges as mountain snows melt in the spring, but the flow slows come summertime. The first popular stop on the route is Covered Bridge Campground, where you can walk across the wooden Albany Covered Bridge, built over the Swift River in 1858 and restored in 1970. The campground's 2½-mile Boulder Loop Trail offers hikers views of the river and of 3,475-foot Mount Chocorua to the south. The Lower Falls Scenic Area is a popular steamy-weather hangout for those who want to sunbathe on the rocks or splash in the shallow pools. It's a great place to watch for whitewater boaters when the river is raging with runoff in the spring.

The cascading Upper Falls at the Rocky Gorge Scenic Area provide a soothing natural soundtrack for sunbathers. Swimming in this steep-walled gorge is not permitted. The Lovequist Loop Trail around Falls Pond is an easy and enjoyable walk in the woods.

Continue the drive west to the Passaconaway Historic Site, where a tour of the Russell Colbath House may leave you shaking your head. Built by sawmill operator Thomas Russell in 1832, the small home was inherited in 1887 by his granddaughter, Ruth Priscilla, and her husband, Thomas Alden Colbath. In 1891, Thomas left the house one day, telling Ruth he would return "in a little while." She hung a lantern in the window every evening—for the ensuing thirty-nine years—as she awaited his return, but she never saw him again. Three years after her death, you'll never guess who showed up. Thomas Colbath's claims to the house were denied, however, and he resumed his rambling ways.

A brief, not-too-strenuous hike of less than half a mile is required to view the narrow flume and series of picturesque waterfalls that make up Sabbaday Falls, one of the Kanc's most popular stops. Back on the highway, your ears may start to pop as you begin the ascent of Mount Kancamagus. Watch for the Sugar Hill, Pemigewasset, and Hancock Overlooks, which all provide a place to park and to appreciate the ruggedly handsome terrain. At first glance, the mountaintops seem to be sporting buzz cuts, but further observation will reveal the articulated pine line of individual evergreens standing proudly atop granite summits. Big Rock

Overleaf: *From the aerial vantage point of Rattlesnake Mountain, daybreak reveals curvaceous and colorful Squam Lake.*

Campground is home to another old-fashioned swimming hole, known as Upper Lady's Bath.

The Kancamagus Highway descends into Lincoln, home of the Loon Mountain Ski Area and several family attractions. Most notable is Clark's Trading Post and its beloved trained bears. In fact, these bears are so well trained, and well fed, that even if they somehow managed to wander off for "a little while," you can bet it wouldn't be forty-two years before they returned.

A Cut Through the Blue
The Lakes Region

ROUTE 22

From Wolfeboro, follow Route 109 North through Melvin Village. Turn right onto Route 171 East to Castle in the Clouds. Reverse on 171 West and rejoin Route 109 North through Moultonborough to Center Sandwich. Watch for a left turn to stay on 109 North at the junction with Route 25, then a right turn to follow 109 North when it breaks away from Route 25. In Center Sandwich, pick up Route 113 West to Holderness.

If you were to let a toddler loose with a pair of scissors and a piece of blue construction paper, he might cut out something that looks a bit like Lake Winnepesaukee. The 72-square-mile lake—New Hampshire's largest—has a convoluted, 182-mile circumference. The many inlets, bays, and secluded coves distort shoreline viewers' perspectives, making the lake seem misleadingly small and intimate. The leftover jagged blue scraps of paper would be fitting, as well, since the Lakes Region is home to more than 270 lakes and ponds.

You'll play a game of peek-a-boo with Winnepesaukee as you drive along the lake's northern shore, starting out from the antique town of Wolfeboro. Situated between Lakes Winnepesaukee and Wentworth, Wolfeboro claims the distinction of being America's first summer resort, because in 1771, Colonial Governor John Wentworth built a summer mansion on the shores of the lake that now bears his name. Today, shops, restaurants, and petite inns flank Winnepesaukee's banks, and visitors can hop aboard Molly the Trolley for a tour of the town's attractions, such as the Libby Museum, which is located on the right as you head north from Wolfeboro on Route 109. Founded in 1912, the natural history museum showcases collections related to Governor Wentworth and the Abenaki tribe. Those who prefer a watery journey can cruise Winnepesaukee on boat tours that push off from Wolfeboro.

As you might have guessed, "Winnepesaukee" is a Native American word. It means "the smile of the Great Spirit." The spirited southern shore of Winnepesaukee brings grins to those who enjoy waterslides, beaches, arcades, jet skis, train rides, and miniature golf, but if a quieter escape makes you beam, the northern shore is surprisingly peaceful, even on peak summer weekends. Route 109 threads between Winnepesaukee and Mirror Lake, passing small farms, stone walls, wooded acres, sleepy marinas, rental cottages, and private homes.

If exploring Lake Winnepesaukee by land and water still does not make your spirit smile, you're in luck: an aerial perspective can be had from the mountaintop Castle in the Clouds. A nearly 2-mile drive off of Route 171 yields spectacular lake and mountain views and ends at the granite-walled mansion that industrialist Thomas Plant named "Lucknow." Built in 1913 at a cost of $7 million, it was an architectural phenomenon that featured unheard of conveniences, such as a central vacuum system and a self-cleaning oven. The 5,200-acre estate offers opportunities to hike to waterfalls, ride horses, and see the Castle Springs water bottling plant in operation.

Back on Route 109 North, watch carefully for Lee Road on the left side, and follow it to a left turn on Lee's Mill Road. The Loon Center at the Frederick and Paula Anna Markus Wildlife Sanctuary, located on Lee's Mill Road, is dedicated to the preservation of habitats for these enigmatic water birds, known for their ability to stay underwater for minutes at a time and for their plaintive, haunting cry. You may encounter a nesting loon if you hike the property's trails during early summer.

As you pass through Moultonborough on the way north, don't miss the mustard and brick red Old Country Store, a town fixture since 1781 and one of the oldest still-operating stores in the country. You could easily spend hours delving into its multiple rooms, which are stockpiled with goodies—penny candy, cheeses, barreled pickles, maple syrup, old-fashioned kitchen utensils, collectibles, toys, and other unexpected treasures. Plunk a quarter into the player piano and be instantly transported to another era. Upstairs, an eclectic collection of Americana includes advertising, farm and household implements, and even a post office, which was located inside the store in the 1800s.

The drive between the classic New England villages of Sandwich and Center Sandwich affords postcard-perfect White Mountains views. You'll pick up Route 113 West just past the Sandwich Fairgrounds, where agriculture and entertainment converge in October, as they have done every year since 1763.

Like Route 109, much of Route 113 is densely treed, so visitors during harvest season are in for a colorful treat. Although you don't see it right away, Route 113 follows the northern shores of Squam Lake, Winnepesaukee's famous cousin. Watch for the trailhead for the Old Bridle Path Trail, which summits Rattlesnake Mountain and leads to dazzling Squam Lake views. It's not a difficult climb, but if you prefer to press on, you can catch a glimpse of Squam Lake—or at least part of it—when you reach Holderness. Like Winnepesaukee, Squam Lake has a rather haphazard shoreline. In fact, Squam's crannies allowed the lake to play the role of a mere pond in the Katharine Hepburn and Henry Fonda film, *On Golden Pond*. Squam Lake Tours in Holderness offers trivia-filled pontoon-boat trips to movie filming locations.

Above: *Lake Winnipesaukee makes an ideal sunset reflecting pool.*

Right: *Inside the Old Country Store in Moultonborough, there's something for everyone—even that impossible relative on your holiday gift list.*

Buds on sugar maples are a telltale sign that spring has reached Hillsborough.

Above: *An independent spirit is omnipresent in New Hampshire, so this patriotically painted Center Sandwich saltbox shouldn't seem surprising.*

Left: *A gaggle of Canada geese chooses a Marlow pond for its pad.*

HILL TOWNS THAT HARBOR HISTORY
HILLSBOROUGH TO PETERBOROUGH,
THE LONG WAY AROUND

ROUTE 23

From the Franklin Pierce Homestead in Hillsborough, turn right and follow Route 31 North. Make the first right onto Shedd Road, and head to Old Carr Bridge at the intersection with Beard Road. Return to Route 31 and continue north through the towns of Windsor and Washington. In Goshen, make a sharp left and head south on Route 10. In Marlow, turn left on Route 123 South and stay on this road when it angles right at a stop sign just past Stoddard. At the junction with Route 9, turn left to continue on Route 123 South. Turn right at a stop sign to continue on Route 123 when it joins Route 202 South to Peterborough.

Franklin Pierce. That name may not ring any bells as you set out on your tour of historic New England, but Pierce, America's fourteenth president, does lay claim to being the only chief executive to hail from New Hampshire. He was a reluctant leader, chosen by fellow Democrats on the forty-ninth ballot after the party failed to coalesce around a candidate in 1852. A grief-stricken Pierce assumed office just a few weeks after witnessing his third and last surviving child killed in a train wreck, and his wife, Jane Means Appleton Pierce, remained sequestered in her sadness throughout his single term in office. She didn't miss much; by most accounts, Pierce's tenure was a poor show that further undermined the stability of a fragile union fiercely divided over slavery.

If Pierce sounds more interesting than you first imagined, you can learn more by making a stop at his childhood home in Hillsborough. This historic mansion was built by his enterprising and politically active father, a Revolutionary War general who rose to the rank of governor of New Hampshire. The Pierce homestead tells many stories. Actually, the costumed interpreters tell the stories, but you might as well get used to absorbing history from your surroundings, as you'll be your own guide for the rest of this drive.

From the Franklin Pierce Homestead, head north on Route 31, but be sure to make your first right onto Shedd Road. At Beard Brook, you'll see the first of three stone-arch bridges along Beard Road. More than a dozen stone bridges were constructed in New Hampshire in the mid nineteenth century, and the five surviving examples are designated National Historic Civil Engineering Landmarks. These graceful spans are held together through the precise cutting and fitting of stones, without the benefit of mortar.

After viewing these feats of architectural engineering, you will wind your way past stone walls and maple farms. Journey through Windsor, southern New Hampshire's smallest town, en route to Washington, which, on December 13, 1776, became the first American town to re-christen itself after George Washington.

Originally settled in 1768 and once a thriving agricultural area, mill town, and railroad-era tourist stop, Washington's population declined to two hundred by 1960, as residents flocked to cities and to better farmlands in the Midwest. Recently, though, the town has been rediscovered by new settlers, who are restoring colonial homes and reinvigorating this historic hill town.

The Washington Common is one of the most photogenic town greens in all of New England. As you face the three crisp-white buildings that guard the green, the 1840 Congregational Church is to the left, the 1787 Town Hall—one of the oldest still in use—is to the right, and sandwiched in between is the building that served as Washington Center School from 1883 to 1993, now the town's police headquarters. Nearby you'll find New Hampshire's first Civil War monument, a gazebo-bandshell, and the 1790 Faxon House, where Sylvanus Thayer, the "father of West Point," spent his youth living with an uncle.

The Washington area is graced with twenty-six lakes and ponds, a few of which you will pass as you continue on toward Goshen. Butterfield Pond is one of four ponds within Pillsbury State Park, which offers forty primitive waterfront campsites. When you reach Goshen, turn south on Route 10. You'll skirt two state forests in Lempster on the way to Marlow. At the junction of Route 10 and Forest Road in Marlow, the often-photographed mill pond reflects three classic white clapboard structures: the 1841 Odd Fellows Hall; the 1829 Marlow United Methodist Church; and Jones Hall, built in 1792 and moved to this site in 1845.

The road from Marlow to Peterborough passes more tiny New Hampshire towns, among them Stoddard, which boasts a country store, lakeside cottages, and a half-mile-long hiking trail. Lined with wild blueberry bushes, the trail leads to the fire tower atop Pitcher Mountain for sweeping views of the Monadnock region. Many Stoddard homes date to the town's boom years of the mid nineteenth century, when four glassworks produced bottles and other glass pieces now highly prized by collectors.

Peterborough may seem like a metropolis compared to the diminutive towns you've been motoring through, but it's still just a town—in fact, it's "Our Town." Pulitzer Prize–winning playwright Thornton Wilder was inspired to write *Our Town* during a stay at the MacDowell Colony in Peterborough. The MacDowell Colony, the nation's oldest artist's colony, has hosted more than ten thousand writers, artists, and composers since 1907. If you have seen or read *Our Town*, you know that the moral is to love life—and appreciate its minutiae—while you're alive. For instance, you now know who Franklin Pierce is, but did you notice on which side he always parted his hair?

The original "dark horse" candidate, Franklin Pierce served as U.S. president from 1853 to 1857. This portrait—showing off his clean left-side part—likely dates from the time of his inauguration. (Photograph courtesy of the Library of Congress. Manuscript Division. The Papers of the Pierce-Aiken Family)

Above: *The cluster of civic buildings surrounding the town common in Washington exudes New England charm. The town hall, at right, dates to 1787 and is one of the nation's oldest town halls still serving its original function.*

Right: *This double-arched bridge in Stoddard, constructed without the benefit of mortar and held together solely through careful shaping and positioning of stones, is one of several built in the Contoocook River Valley during the first half of the nineteenth century. Today, the area's surviving stone bridges are considered engineering marvels.*

Periwinkles, marine snails with characteristic whorled shells, thrive in tidepools such as this one in Rye.

Ocean breezes tickle dune grasses at Hampton Beach. The beach is uncharacteristically serene without its summer contingent of sun seekers.

The New Hampshire Marine Memorial casts a protective gaze over Hampton Beach. The statue was dedicated in 1957 and inscribed in memory of "New Hampshire's historic war dead . . . lost at sea in defence of our country."

A COMPACT COASTLINE
HAMPTON BEACH TO NEW CASTLE

ROUTE 24

From Hampton Beach, follow Route 1A North. North of Rye, watch for a right turn at a stop sign to stay on Route 1A North. Turn right shortly thereafter and follow Route 1B to New Castle.

You have to live in New England to fully appreciate that the changing of the seasons is more than just the rise and fall of temperatures and the shifting colors of the foliage. This drive along New Hamsphire's compact, 18-mile shoreline illustrates the striking impact that seasonality can have. Three seasons of the year, it is a quiet backroads jaunt; the fourth, it is a parking lot.

Summer is, of course, the peak season in coastal communities throughout New England. With just a petite strip of ocean frontage, much of it accessible to the public, southern New Hampshire experiences a massive influx of summer sun seekers. Hampton Beach State Park, where this trip begins, is the most crowded hot-weather hangout. If you stroll the boardwalk in season, you may have to just take it on faith that there really are miles of sand here; the beige granules can be almost totally obscured beneath a rainbow sea of beach umbrellas, blankets, and towels. Hampton Beach is an old-fashioned family beach resort—replete with no-frills motels, tacky souvenir stores, arcades, and diminutive beach cottages situated spitting distance apart. When summer ends, the scent of fried dough finally dissipates, the shops and food stalls shutter, the sandy expanse is once again revealed, and parking is no longer at a premium.

As you follow the coastline north from Hampton Beach, the waterfront on the right remains primarily state-owned public beach, while on the left side of the road, you'll begin to see higher-priced rentals, condos, and private homes, including architectural marvels with angled facades and spindly legs designed to maximize the coveted ocean views. North Beach and North Hampton State Beach are a bit quieter than Hampton Beach, with narrower strips of sand and a bit more vigorous surf. In Rye, Jenness State Beach is a good family spot for swimming and sandcastle building; the beachless Rye Harbor State Park provides opportunities for boat-watching, saltwater fishing, and picnicking; and the beach at Wallis Sands State Park is a baking sheet for bronzed bodies on clear summer days. A bit farther north, Odiorne State Park encompasses the largest undeveloped tract of New Hampshire's coast, a rocky stretch of shore with thick vegetation and an artificial pond and marsh. In addition to providing a protected habitat for a variety of wildlife, the park also preserves remnants of coastal fortifications erected during World War II. Odiorne Point was purchased by the federal government in 1942 as the site for Fort Dearborn, a military complex critical to the defense of Portsmouth Harbor and its naval shipyard. You can learn more about the natural and human history of Odiorne Point and the adjacent seacoast at the Seacoast Science Center, located within the park.

The island of New Castle is home to another historic fort that was built to protect the harbor. Fort Constitution, originally called Fort William and Mary, was established by the British in the 1600s. In 1774, it was raided by colonists in one of the first acts of defiance against the crown. The brick and stone fort was reconstructed and expanded on the site in 1808, and today, at Fort Constitution Historic Site, you can explore what remains of it. You'll also see Portsmouth Harbor Light, also known as Fort Point Light. Portsmouth citizens, concerned about navigation around New Castle island, first began petitioning for a lighthouse in 1765. The wooden beacon erected here in 1771 was the tenth lighthouse built in the American colonies. The current cast-iron structure has illuminated the entrance to Portsmouth Harbor since 1877. The lighthouse remains an active navigation aid, and visitors are allowed inside during occasional open houses.

If it's a leisurely scenic drive you seek, this route is best avoided during the high season. If you're here in the summertime, start out early, pack plenty of cold beverages and an ounce or two of patience, and you'll be treated to soothing views of the sparkling Atlantic, albeit frequently teeming with bobbing bathers. Better yet, plan your visit for Labor Day weekend and the day or two after. You'll get two vacation experiences for the price of one and see just how abruptly the seasons can change in New England.

Although it has the shortest shoreline of any state on the Atlantic coast, New Hampshire's beaches have long been popular summertime playgrounds. The Hampton Beach trolley unloads a mass of beachgoers circa 1910. (Photograph courtesy of the New Hampshire Historical Society)

PART VI

MAINE:
NEW ENGLAND "IN THE ROUGH"

Facing page: *Lobster boats fill the waters of Bass Harbor, a quaint coastal village on the "quiet side" of Mount Desert Island.*

Above: *Baxter State Park is an ideal choice for a Maine moose safari. The abundant wetland plants serve as an all-you-can-eat salad bar for moose with the munchies, such as this mama, papa, and yearling.*

Whether elegantly inscribed among the offerings of a fine Portland restaurant or scribbled on the blackboard outside a roadside shack hundreds of miles inland, Maine's signature shellfish shows up on menus statewide. You haven't truly experienced the joy of lobster, though, until you've eaten it "in the rough." Forget fancy table linens and sparkling wine goblets. Lobster tastes best when consumed in rustic environs—outdoors at a picnic table, salty breezes scattering your big stack of napkins, and only rudimentary tools to augment your bare hands as you devour this tasty crustacean. Fashion must take a backseat, too, as a plastic lobster bib is a must if you want to avoid a buttery mishap.

Lobster isn't the only thing Maine serves up "in the rough." The least densely populated state east of the Mississippi—a sprawling northern expanse roughly equal in area to the other five New England states combined—remains in many ways a frontier land. Sure, today's pioneers arrive in SUVs with skis or kayaks strapped to roofs instead of in Conestoga wagons laden with all of life's possessions. Still, the sense of seeking adventure in uncharted realms remains strong.

The outlet stores and sandy beaches of the southern shore quickly yield to rugged rockbound coast. Thread the mighty Mississippi, Amazon, Yangtze, and Nile Rivers together, and Maine's 32,000 miles of rivers and streams would outrun them. Venture inland and northward, and you'll relinquish the right of way to moose and logging trucks. You'll also encounter places with names such as TA R2 WELS among the state's 424 "unorganized townships" that are too sparsely populated to warrant jurisdiction.

Yet for all of Maine's uninhabited tracts, raging rapids, rocky ocean breakers, glacier-scarred mountain peaks, and bumpy dirt roads, a gentleness lurks beneath this coarse exterior. You'll see it in the first rosy blush of sunrise, which reaches the state's eastern edge earlier than anywhere else in the United States. You'll hear it in the mystic cry of a lonesome loon on one of Maine's countless lakes. You'll breathe it in the woodsy aroma of forested hills or in cold, saline-infused shoreline gusts. You'll feel it in the rhythmic lilt of a carriage pulled along roads forever closed to cars. You'll taste it, of course, in the sweet freshness of the state's signature shellfish. However rustic the setting, there's truly nothing rough about eating just-caught lobster, save perhaps realizing you've savored the final morsel.

LOBSTER AND LIGHTHOUSES
MAINE'S SOUTHERN SHORE

Three New England icons engender a fervor that cannot easily be explained to the uninitiated: leaves, lighthouses, and lobsters. Southern Maine can't rival the rest of the state for fabulous fall foliage, but for luscious crustaceans and majestic towers of light, you won't find a more ideal destination. A camera and a cooler outfitted with freezer packs or bagged ice

ROUTE 25

Follow 1A North through York Village to a right on Route 103 West to Fort McClary. Double back on 103 East and return to 1A North. Turn right onto Nubble Road, then right on Sohier Park Road to Nubble Light. Follow Sohier Road back to a right on Nubble Road and continue along the shore. Turn left on Broadway, then right to continue on 1A North. Bear right to follow Shore Road through Ogunquit. Turn right and follow Route 1 North. In Wells, turn right on Bourne Avenue, left on Ocean Avenue, and right on Webhannet Road. At the road's end, turn right for Wells Beach or continue by turning left onto Mile Road. Turn right on Route 1 North. Bear right and follow Route 9 East through Kennebunkport. At Cape Porpoise, where Route 9 turns left, go straight onto Pier Road.

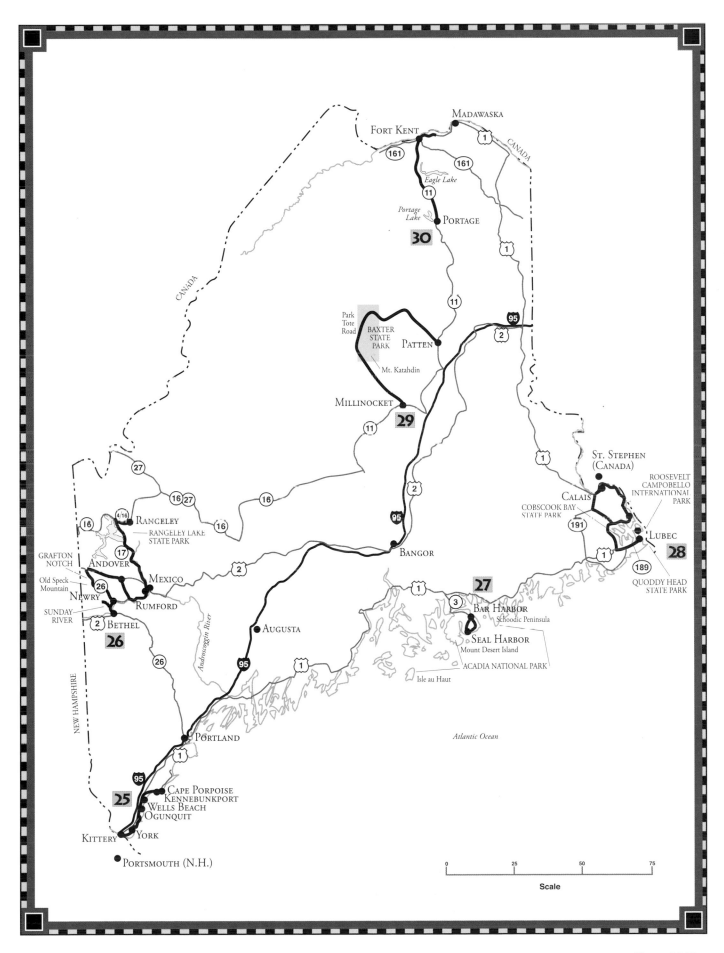

MADAWASKA

FORT KENT

161

161

Eagle Lake

11

Portage
Lake

PORTAGE

30

1

1

11

Park
Tote
Road

BAXTER
STATE
PARK

95

2

PATTEN

Mt. Katahdin

MILLINOCKET

29

11

1

ST. STEPHEN
(CANADA)

ROOSEVELT
CAMPOBELLO
INTERNATIONAL
PARK

27

16 27

16

27

16

CALAIS

COBSCOOK BAY
STATE PARK

191

LUBEC

28

RANGELEY

RANGELEY LAKE
STATE PARK

4/16

16

17

2

95

189

QUODDY HEAD
STATE PARK

GRAFTON
NOTCH

ANDOVER

Old Speck
Mountain

26

MEXICO

NEWRY

RUMFORD

SUNDAY
RIVER

2

BETHEL

26

BANGOR

2

Androscoggin River

AUGUSTA

1

3

BAR HARBOR

Schoodic Peninsula

SEAL HARBOR

Mount Desert Island

ACADIA NATIONAL PARK

Isle au Haut

26

95

1

Atlantic Ocean

NEW HAMPSHIRE

PORTLAND

1

95

CAPE PORPOISE
KENNEBUNKPORT

WELLS BEACH

OGUNQUIT

25

KITTERY

YORK

PORTSMOUTH (N.H.)

0   25   50   75

Scale

Located off the coast of Kittery, the granite block Whaleback Ledge Light is Maine's southernmost lighthouse.

Above: *Lobster tastes best when eaten "in the rough" at one of Maine's many seafood shacks. The appointments may be rustic, but the catch is definitely fresh.*

Left: *The Wiggley Bridge, a unique cable suspension bridge spanning the York River, has been a York landmark since the early 1900s.*

(lobsters and freshwater don't mix) are mandatory gear. So is a great deal of patience if you're driving this route during the congested summer season, when this trip might be best split over two days. You'll need to exercise some restraint, too, and resist pulling off the road at the first hand-painted "live lobsters" sign you see; your clawed companions can't wait in the car too long as you explore the region's diverse offerings.

Your first stop is Kittery's Fort McClary State Historic Site, which played a role in Maine's military defense from the colonial era through the twentieth century. Although it was in operation during six wars—the Revolutionary War, War of 1812, Civil War, Spanish-American War, and both World Wars—the fort saw little military action. Today, the block-house and other historic structures represent different periods of construction, which happened as the fort was upgraded to meet the changing needs of the military and the defense of Maine's southern coastline. From the fort, you can look out across Portsmouth Harbor to spot Whaleback Light. The 50-foot granite lighthouse, built in 1872, was the third beacon situated on this rocky outcropping. It remains an active aid to navigation.

Before heading to the second lighthouse on this tour, which you will observe up close, two stops merit consideration. The Wiggley Bridge, located on the north side of Route 103, leads to the Stedman Woods bird sanctuary. The unique 104-foot suspension cable footbridge spanning the York River was originally built in the early 1900s. Back on the seashore, Harbor Beach in York Harbor offers the choice of a sandy stroll or a more challenging rocky hike aside the Atlantic.

Sohier Park is the prime viewing point for one of Maine's best-loved and most photographed lighthouses. The Cape Neddick or "Nubble" Light and its crimson-roofed Victorian keeper's house were built in 1879. The lighthouse is at its loveliest when illuminated with strings of white lights for the holiday season.

The back way to Ogunquit on Shore Road takes you past pebbly beaches, stalwart cliffs, and stately homes. None has a view more spectacular than the historic Cliff House perched atop Bald Head Cliff. In operation since 1872, the resort is an inviting place to pause for lunch or light refreshments at a table from which you can overlook and overhear the convergence of cliffs and sea.

Shore Road continues through the heart of Ogunquit, where galleries, inns, cafés, piano bars, boutiques, and beaches bustle during the summer season but suffer from off-season inertia. First tread by indigenous peoples, the famed Marginal Way is a $1\frac{1}{4}$-mile seaside walkway that begins in the center of Ogunquit and connects it to the fishing village of Perkins Cove.

Shore Road ends at Route 1, the main drag through Maine's South Coast region. Fear not. In Wells, you can resume your backroad journey along the ocean en route to Wells Beach, a family-sized sandbox around which a plethora of pastel-painted beach cottages has sprouted. If you've had enough sun and sand, other activities in this corner of coastline include antiquing, birding, and exploring the vibrant village of Kennebunkport. Treasure hunters will find dozens of antique shops along Route 1 in Wells. The trails and observation decks at the Rachel Carson National Wildlife Refuge allow birdwatchers to spy on migratory birds within a protected habitat of tidal marshes, estuaries, and forests. Kennebunkport has been a vibrant commercial hub for centuries, and it is perhaps best known as the summer home of George and Barbara Bush.

With whale watches, beaches, historic sea captains' homes, gift shops galore, pubs, auction houses, art galleries, museums, walking tours, restaurants, and sightseeing cruises, there is plenty to tempt you to conclude your drive in Kennebunkport, but forge on to Cape Porpoise, which lies just on the other side of town. First discovered in the 1600s and named by Captain John Smith, the cape remains an authentic working harbor. You can amble along the docks for a glimpse of the Maine of yesteryear, when the hard work of fishing and lobstering sustained coastal communities. From the docks, you can see one more lighthouse, Goat Island Light, which has cast its protective beam over these waters since 1859, after replacing its 1822 predecessor. Best of all, your patience has finally paid off. The lobsters you buy in Cape Porpoise are just in from the Atlantic. To get fresher lobster, you'd have to move to Maine, buy a boat, pay a fee, and ace the Non-commercial Lobster License test.

GO FOR THE GOLD
MOUNTAINS AND LAKES OF WESTERN MAINE

Winter brings skiers and snowboarders with Olympic dreams. Endless fields of sunny dandelions sprout in the spring. Summer's glitter sparkles on the surface of more than one hundred ponds and lakes. And autumn electroplates mountainsides with a golden luster. If that's not enough to entice you to return to the lakes and peaks of western Maine season after season, perhaps the prospect of finding your own nugget of gold is.

The riches of this region can't all be measured in karats, though. As this drive climbs and coasts through mountain notches and along riverbanks and lakeshores, you'll be rewarded with covered bridges, waterfalls, spectacular vistas, and maybe even a moose or two.

Set out from Bethel, a town with bountiful resources for visitors to Sunday River and other local ski areas. There's also no shortage of historical structures; forty-seven of the town's buildings are incorporated into the Broad Street Historic District, a 370-acre area along Broad, Church, and Park Streets that is included on the National Register of Historical Places. Bethel is also the Maine town with the heartiest sense of humor. For instance, in 1999, the town came together to build the world's tallest snowman; Angus stood 113 feet, 7 inches tall. Every year, Sunday River's Santa Sunday brings out more than two hundred red-suit-clad skiers.

ROUTE 26

From Bethel, follow Route 26 North. Turn left on Sunday River Road, and follow covered bridge signs; the road turns to the right before reaching Sunday River Bridge on the left. Reverse back to Route 26 and continue north by turning left. In Newry, turn left to stay on 26 North through Grafton Notch. Turn right on East B Hill Road and then right on Route 5 South at a stop sign in Andover. Turn left on Covered Bridge Road and drive across the Lovejoy Covered Bridge. Reverse and continue south on Route 5, then turn left onto Route 2 East through Rumford. Turn left to stay on Route 2 before the bridge over the Androscoggin River. At the rotary, follow signs to stay on Route 2, then watch for an immediate left turn to continue on 2 North. At a traffic light, turn right to stay on Route 2, then make a left at the first light onto Route 17 West. At the end of 17, turn right and follow Route 4 to Rangeley.

Above: *Route 17 follows the shore of Beaver Pond, one of the string of lakes and ponds in the Rangeley region that add to the area's allure as a prime leaf-peeping destination.*

Right: *At 70 feet in length, the Lovejoy Bridge over the Ellis River in South Andover is the shortest of Maine's nine covered bridges.*

Above: *The non-denominational Union Log Church in Oquossoc was built entirely of spruce logs in 1916.*

Left: *A stop at Height of Land overlooking Mooselookmeguntic Lake is a sensory experience at any time of year but especially in summer when the scent of pearly everlasting is oddly reminiscent of maple syrup.*

Angus, the World's Tallest Snowman, loomed large over the town of Bethel in 1999. The 113-foot, 7-inch frozen giant was made of 9 million pounds of snow and sported two 10-foot evergreens for arms and a pair of 4-foot wreaths for eyes. (Photo courtesy of the Bethel Area Chamber of Commerce, Bethel, Maine)

And the annual North American Wife Carrying Championships reward the winning chap with his wife's weight in liquid gold—beer. There's always something lighthearted happening in Bethel.

More history-laden scenery is to be found on Sunday River Road in Newry. The Sunday River Bridge, built in 1872, is nicknamed the Artist's Bridge because it is Maine's most painted and photographed covered bridge. The wooden span is closed to vehicular traffic, but there is ample room to park and walk across.

Route 26 follows the Bear River through Grafton Notch, and this picturesque channel through the Mahoosuc Range is popular with leaf peepers. Your windshield will beautifully frame images of Old Speck, the third highest mountain in Maine. The Appalachian Trail, which traverses the notch, climbs Old Speck on the way to its northern terminus in Baxter State Park.

Before you enter Grafton Notch State Park, keep your eyes open for a tiny sign on the right for Wight Brook. From there, you can hike a dirt path alongside Step Falls, a graduated series of watery cascades stepping Slinky-like over rocks. This well-hidden property is owned by the Maine Chapter of The Nature Conservancy. Don't beat yourself up if you miss Step Falls, though. Grafton Notch's most dramatic waterfall, Screw Auger Falls, is well marked and just ahead on the left. Unlike Step Falls, which requires a hike, Screw Auger Falls can be seen from fenced-in observation areas that are a short walk from the parking lot. As you continue north, you'll also spot signs for Mother Walker Falls, a 100-foot series of cascades. Trails lead to scenic waterfall overlooks.

The once-paved but now-bumpy East B Hill Road leads through a heavily treed, narrow concourse that will deposit you in Andover, where you'll pick up Route 5 South. A left off Route 5 at Covered Bridge Road allows you to drive across Maine's shortest covered bridge. The Lovejoy Covered Bridge, built in 1868, spans the Ellis River.

As you meander along the Androscoggin River to Rumford, an old paper mill town, and then north along the Swift River toward Rangeley, be ready to stomp on the brakes and grab the camera. You're in prime moose-viewing country. The Swift River is where gold was first discovered in Maine in the early eighteenth century. No fooling—you can still find gold here. If you're feeling lucky, stop at Coos Canyon in Byron, a popular place to pan for precious metal. A shop opposite the striated gorge has prospecting gear for rent, although packing a perforated pie plate from home is a perfectly acceptable alternative.

If you don't strike it rich, or even if you do, continue along Route 17 West, and as the road climbs, watch carefully for unmarked pullovers on the left. These stops are situated at a spot known as "Height of Land," which affords priceless views of Mooselookmeguntic Lake flowing around Toothaker Island and blending with Cupsuptic Lake beyond. New Hampshire's White Mountains are visible in the misty distance. Mother Nature repaints this panorama with each new season with dabs of snowy white, velvety greens, and intense reds, oranges, and golds.

There's one treasure left to see before you call it a day—Rangeley Lake, the 10-square-mile water body at the center of this region's more than one hundred lakes and ponds. Rangeley Lake scenic overlooks and the entrance to Rangeley Lake State Park are designated on the right side of Route 17. The park provides areas for swimming, fishing for salmon and trout, and camping alongside the tranquil waters. When you reach the end of Route 17, turn right; you'll continue to flirt with the lake as you follow Route 4 to the town of Rangeley. Originally a small logging and farming outpost, Rangeley became a booming sportsmen's paradise in the second half of the nineteenth century. Private cabins and homes have replaced most of the grand hotels and sporting camps of the area's heyday. If you found a few sizable nuggets back at Coos Canyon, you might be able to afford a down payment.

Off in the distance, Otter Cliffs in Acadia National Park stands 110 feet high above the relentlessly pummeling Atlantic surf.

PARADISE PRESERVED
ACADIA NATIONAL PARK

ROUTE 27

From Bar Harbor, follow Route 3 West to the Acadia National Park Visitor Center in Hulls Cove. Follow the Park Loop Road through Acadia and, near Eagle Lake, turn right onto Cadillac Mountain Summit Road. Ascend the 3.5-mile road to the summit, then descend and turn right, following the Park Loop Road back to Route 3.

Maine's 80,000-acre Mount Desert (pronounced "dessert") Island—named *L'Isle des Monts Deserts*, or "The Island of Bare Mountains" in 1604 by French explorer Samuel de Champlain—is the third-largest isle off the east coast of the United States. But don't expect it to be anything like its larger, Atlantic-encircled companions, Long Island and Martha's Vineyard. For starters, it's home to twenty-six dome-shaped forested mountain peaks, including the highest point on the eastern seaboard north of Brazil. It's also largely owned by you, the public.

Acadia National Park's more than 47,000 acres, encompassing 30,300 acres on Mount Desert Island along with large tracts on Isle au Haut and the mainland Schoodic Peninsula, were a remarkable gift from private citizens to the American people. Long before glossy brochures, the island's first tourists were enticed by the dramatic wilderness portrayed in the landscape paintings of Thomas Cole and Frederic Church. By 1880, more than thirty hotels had sprung up to serve the island's summer influx. Soon after, the rugged seaside resort attracted wealthy seasonal residents with names like Rockefeller, Morgan, Ford, Astor, Vanderbilt, and Pulitzer. Concerned for the future of their island paradise, these well-to-do settlers established a public land trust in 1901. The trust was overseen by George Bucknam Dorr, who invested incredible money and energy over the ensuing forty-three years to ensure the preservation of and public access to this natural wonderland. In 1919, Lafayette National Park became the first national park east of the Mississippi and the first comprised entirely of lands donated by private property owners. It was renamed Acadia in 1929.

Though most of the island's elite lost their "Millionaire's Row" homes in a 1947 fire that raged for ten days and engulfed 17,000 acres, the park survives as a testament to their generosity and foresight. A few surviving grand cottages are now inns in Bar Harbor, the natural home base for visitors to Acadia. Known as Eden until 1796—not for the Biblical garden of paradise but for English statesman Sir Richard Eden—Bar Harbor is a laidback yet lively former fishing village with tourist amenities aplenty.

From Bar Harbor, Acadia National Park is reached via Route 3 West. The Hulls Cove Visitor Center offers maps, recorded audio tours, and other orientation materials. Entrance passes may be purchased here or at a station near the start of the Park Loop Road. The Park Loop is a 20-mile sightseeing circuit that unveils Acadia in dramatic fashion. Both the road and the visitor center are closed in winter, but the park remains open, and the loop can be traversed by snowmobile.

Though it doesn't cover many miles, the Park Loop Road can occupy a full day's drive. Traffic and the speed limit will slow you, but not as much as your desire to unleash your seatbelt and explore unfettered the omnipresent beauty along the route as it climbs from shore to summit.

The power of Acadia lies in the sounds and scenes that arise from the juxtaposition of sea and mountain-spiked shore. From the first parking area overlooking island-freckled Frenchman Bay, you may decide that you don't want to miss a single pullover along the loop, and there are plenty of natural attractions and scenic vantage points. If you do have to make choices, these are the must-sees.

At the 1947 Fire Overlook, you'll see the birch, aspen, and oak forest that now thrives where spruce-fir dominated before the great conflagration. Crowds congregate at Sand Beach, and parking is tight in July and August. The sand is composed of pulverized seashells and marine creatures. Only a few brave souls use this as a swimming beach, since the water temperature rarely rises above 55 degrees. Just under a mile up the road, Thunder Hole entertains visitors when the tide is right and the waves are voluminous, particularly after a storm. In optimum conditions, water can spout as high as 40 feet in an enormous, thundering blast as air and water are forced through a small natural cavern. The Otter Cliffs area is a fine place to leave the busy Park Loop Road for a saunter along the high bedrock walls. As you follow Ocean Path to Otter Point, watch for a bell buoy marking an offshore rock known as "the Spindle." Samuel de Champlain would have appreciated that buoy; he ran his ship into the Spindle while exploring the coastline of the isle he named. A stop for afternoon tea at Jordan Pond House has been a tradition since the late 1800s. Although the original Pond House burned in 1979, the main attractions remain unchanged: crisp, airy popovers served with jam and romantic views of "the Bubbles," softly rounded twin mountains that reflect in Jordan Pond.

As you encounter Eagle Lake north of Jordan Pond, look for the right-hand turnoff for the Cadillac Mountain Summit Road. This 7-mile roundtrip detour will take you 1,530 feet above the sea, to the highest point on America's eastern shore, where the climate is subalpine and glaciers are to blame for the haphazardly deposited boulder debris on Cadillac Mountain. You can credit the icy invaders with most of the marvelous features etched into the landscape below, too. The Summit Road, which opened to auto traffic in 1931, is also your escape route for descending Cadillac's pink granite slopes.

Once you've closed the loop, remember that Acadia offers 120 miles of hiking trails; 57 miles of carriage roads accessible to pedestrians, horses, skiers, and cyclists; and sixteen lakes and ponds open to watercraft. Even without wandering far from the Park Loop Road, there are as many ways to embrace and explore Acadia as there are individuals who visit this geologically and biologically diverse enclave. Seek out a piece of paradise that calls to you—a rocky perch overlooking the rolling ocean, a quiet forest footpath, a cobblestone bridge along a manicured carriage road, a craggy mountain ledge, or a pondside patch of grass—and truly make Acadia your own.

Right: *Clouds check their appearance in the mirror of Eagle Lake, as dawn's early light illuminates the pink granite slopes of Cadillac Mountain.*

Below: *The Jordan Pond House offers romantic views of "the Bubbles," a pair of gently rounded peaks that floats above Jordan Pond.*

Left: *The summit of Cadillac Mountain, the highest point on the East Coast, has been accessible to motorists since 1931.*

Below: *Acadia National Park's elaborate system of carriage roads includes seventeen gracefully arched bridges constructed of hand-hewn granite.*

The Rockefeller Carriage Roads offer a scenic backroad route for exploring Acadia National Park and Mount Desert Island. (Photograph courtesy of the Library of Congress, Prints and Photographs Division, Historic American Engineering Record; photograph by Jet Lowe, 1994)

The Park Loop Road through Acadia National Park provides easy access to many of Mount Desert Island's scenic wonders. Construction of the asphalt concourse was funded in part by John D. Rockefeller Jr., a summer resident of Seal Harbor, but his heart and his wallet were more heavily invested in Acadia's other road system—the one that you can't drive.

From 1913 to 1940, Rockefeller oversaw the design and development of seventeen stone bridges and 57 miles of finely engineered, broken-stone carriage roads that lead to some of the island's most enchanting interior spots and climb high along mountain ridges. Today, Rockefeller's cherished carriage roads, his gift to the nation along with more than 10,000 acres of land, are maintained by the National Park Service for use by hikers, cyclists, and cross-country skiers. If you want an authentic experience of the lifestyle Rockefeller hoped to preserve at the advent of the automobile age, call Wildwood Stables and reserve a spot on a carriage tour. Private carriage charters may also be booked. The leisurely, clip-clopping pace of a team of Percherons or Belgian draft horses is the optimum speed at which to savor Acadia. Wildwood Stables is located on the Park Loop Road, just south of the Jordan Pond House.

ROUTE 28

From Quoddy Head State Park in Lubec, follow South Lubec Road to Route 189. Turn left on Route 189 West toward Whiting, and turn right onto Route 1 North. Follow Route 1 to Calais, turning left in town to stay on Route 1. In Baring, turn left on Route 191 and head south to a left on Route 214 toward Pembroke. Cross Route 1, turn right on Old County Road, left onto Leighton Point Road, then right on Clarkside Road and follow it to the end. Turn left onto Reversing Falls Road, a dirt road that leads to Mahar Point overlooking the Cobscook Reversing Falls.

FIRST LIGHT DRIVE
DOWNEAST MAINE

As the sun rouses America from its slumber each morning, the first wake-up call comes to tiny Lubec, Maine, the easternmost town in the United States. Founded in 1811, this coastal community once thrived on ship-building and sardine smoking, but today, its main claim to fame is its location at the "Beginning of America." It's also the perfect place from which to embark on a voyage through the heart of "Downeast Maine," a moniker that originated with sailors from Boston, who had to sail downwind and to the east to reach Maine's northern harbors due to the prevailing southwest winds.

To experience the first blush of sunrise, start your day in Quoddy Head State Park, where West Quoddy Head Light, a distinctive, candy cane–striped beacon overlooking the Bay of Fundy, guards the country's easternmost point of land. The light station was established in 1808, and the 1858 replacement tower and its original Fresnel lens remain on duty, warning mariners away from this rocky promontory. Exhibits at the visitor center detail the history of the much-photographed brick lighthouse, which has sported anywhere from six to eight horizontal red stripes through various repaintings. The surrounding 532-acre state park features picnic sites; hiking trails through spruce forests and rare-plant-inhabited bogs; and opportunities for bird, whale, seal, and tide watching.

If the Old Columbian Store on Route 189 is open, be sure to stop in before you leave Lubec. The company store that served employees of the Columbian Sardine Packing plant during the first half of the twentieth century now houses the Lubec Historical Society and a variety of intriguing exhibits. A few perpetual yard sales dot the route to Whiting, but the real attraction—at least if you're traveling this route during northern Maine's staccato blooming season—is the proliferation of variegated roadside wildflowers.

The road from Whiting to Calais provides glimpses of wild Maine. About 6 miles south of Dennysville, Cobscook Bay State Park, named for a Maliseet-Passamaquoddy Indian word meaning "boiling tides," is surrounded on three sides by saltwater bays renowned for their remarkably high tides, which average 24 feet and can surge as high as 28 feet. When the tides subside, campers comb the shore in search of soft-shell clams. Inland to the west, the Edmunds Division of the Moosehorn National Wildlife Refuge is a 7,200-acre protected habitat for wildlife, including more than two hundred bird species.

The town of Perry is located halfway between the equator and the North Pole, but before you get there you'll have the option of detouring south on Route 190 to Eastport, the easternmost city in the nation. The small port city is located on Moose Island, which is connected to the mainland by a short causeway. Fish and mustard may seem an odd combination, but Eastport is both a producer of millions of pounds of farm-raised salmon and home to Raye's Old Stone Mustard Mill, which has produced stone-ground mustard since 1903. Stop by to tour the mill when it is in operation and sample some of the Raye family's zesty condiments.

Back on Route 1 North, you'll soon reach Calais, located across the St. Croix River from the Canadian town of St. Stephen. The first settlers reached Calais in the 1770s, but St. Croix Island, located 8 miles offshore, was settled by a party of Frenchmen led by Samuel de Champlain in 1604— three years before the English established their colony at Jamestown, Virginia. Calais and St. Stephen jointly celebrate a week-long International Festival each August.

This journey's loop concludes at Pembroke, the site of the natural wonder known as the Cobscook Reversing Falls. This swirling whitewater tidal rip is created by the convergence of Dennys Bay, Whiting Bay, and Cobscook Bay in a narrow tidal channel. Tide changes at the reversing falls occur more than an hour later than what is stated for Eastport; the most impressive time to see the falls perform its reversing act is at about two hours prior to high tide.

Downeast Maine will always be awakened early, but after this long day's drive, feel free to pull the curtains and put the sun on snooze tomorrow.

Lubec bids the sun adieu as it dips below the horizon.

The narrow Lubec Channel is all that separates Maine from New Brunswick, Canada. The 1885 Mulholland Light (now inactive) is the only lighthouse jointly owned by the United States and Canada, as it sits within the Roosevelt Campobello International Park.

Orange hawkweed, deep and pale purple lupines, and other perennial wildflowers stack up like a dense floral layer cake alongside roadways in Downeast Maine.

From the black sand beaches of Quoddy Head State Park, it is possible to spot whales and seals cavorting offshore.

You'll have to leave the country and the time zone, but when you're in Lubec, Maine, you'd be remiss if you didn't make the short drive across the FDR International Bridge to Canada's Campobello Island, the beloved summer retreat of Franklin Delano Roosevelt. The New Brunswick island hideaway emerged as a summer vacationland for wealthy American families in the latter half of the nineteenth century, and James and Sara Roosevelt took one-year-old Franklin to the island in 1883 for the first of many annual summer escapes.

You can tour the thirty-four-room, cedar-shingled cottage owned by the Roosevelts, now preserved within the Roosevelt Campobello International Park, a memorial to the president jointly owned and operated by the U.S. and Canada. It was at Campobello that a thirty-nine-year-old FDR contracted polio during the summer of 1921. The debilitating disease and a burgeoning political career would prevent him from returning to Campobello for a dozen years, and he made only three brief additional visits during his lifetime.

If you have time to venture to the northern tip of the island, you can view the wooden, octagonal East Quoddy Light, built in 1829 and painted with a unique red cross design. Though it is possible to walk out to the lighthouse at low tide, be forewarned that once the tide comes in, you could be stranded for as long as eight hours.

Ready for a round of golf, a young Franklin stands near the Roosevelt family home on Campobello Island, circa 1899. (Photo courtesy of the Franklin D. Roosevelt Presidential Library and Museum, Hyde Park, New York)

FOREVER WILD
BAXTER STATE PARK

ROUTE 29

From Baxter State Park Headquarters on Balsam Drive in Millinocket, follow Central Street (Routes 11 and 157) northwest to a right on Katahdin Avenue. Curve left onto Bates Street, which becomes Millinocket Road. Enter Baxter State Park and follow the Park Tote Road 41 miles through the park. Exit the park on Grand Lake Road, which becomes Route 159 to Patten.

By modern standards anyway, Percival P. Baxter was an odd kid. It wasn't all that strange that the seven-year-old grew impatient while on a fishing outing with his dad on a cool and damp day. Things got interesting, though, when James Phinney Baxter promised to pay his son $10 per pound for the next fish over five pounds he caught. Young Percival perked up, cast his line, and almost immediately reeled in an eight-pound spotted trout. When asked what he would do with his $80 prize, a small fortune in 1884, the peculiar tot responded that he was going to sock it away in a savings account.

By the time of his death in 1969, Percival P. Baxter's fish account had grown to more than $1,000, and he bequeathed the money to Maine's Inland Fisheries and Wildlife Department for fish research. This donation was a mere cherry atop Baxter's contributions to the preservation of Maine's natural wonders. During his two terms as state governor, Baxter was mostly thwarted in his efforts to protect Maine's northern forests, so in 1930, he took matters into his own hands. Beginning with the purchase of 6,000 acres of logging lands surrounding and including Mount Katahdin, Baxter acquired parcel after parcel, deeding the land to the state with the strict stipulation that it remain forever wild. He also established a $7 million trust for maintenance of the park. As a result, Baxter State Park remains financially independent to this day, with no public tax dollars used to maintain the park, and it is also an independent state agency separate from Maine's Bureau of Parks and Lands.

Mile-high Katahdin, the state's highest peak, is the pièce de résistance within Baxter State Park's 204,733 acres. The first stunning view of the mighty mountain, often draped mysteriously in fog and sporting a cap of white snowdust, comes as you wind northwest from the small paper company town of Millinocket toward the park's south entrance. Baxter State Park Headquarters in Millinocket is a good place to pick up a park map. Remember to check your gas gauge before heading out of town.

The 41-mile Park Tote Road, alternately known as the Wilderness Tote Road or Nesowadnehunk Tote Road, is the main vehicular passageway through the park. The road, first blazed for horse-driven wagons supplying lumbering and sporting camps, is mostly dirt and has a 20 mph speed limit. Motorcycles, motor homes, and trailers over a certain size are prohibited. You may feel as though you're driving on a washboard for the

Seven-year-old Percival P. Baxter poses proudly with the eight-pound spotted trout that launched his lifetime effort to preserve Maine's fish and wildlife and the wilderness they inhabit. (Photograph courtesy of the Baxter State Park Archives)

two-plus hours it takes to cover these 41 miles. Keeping the road unpaved was part of Baxter's wilderness ideal, so as to encourage hiking instead of driving, and, in fact, the park is prohibited from improving the road. Baxter, himself an animal lover, also put in place a restriction against pets on the trails in order to protect the area's wildlife.

If you choose to follow some of the intriguing offshoots from the main road, or if you get out of the car to hike some of the 200 miles of trails that crisscross the park and climb to the tops of its forty-six mountain peaks and ridges, you can easily spend a full day at Baxter. Overnight wilderness camping is limited to one thousand people, and reservations are required.

Shortly after passing through the Togue Pond Gatehouse, you'll be presented with your first fork in the road. While the Park Tote Road heads to the left, Roaring Brook Road extends to the right. This 8-mile, dead-end offshoot accesses a picnic area, campground, and trails leading to Sandy Stream Pond, up South Turner Mountain, and to the summit of Katahdin. At the summit, the Knife Edge trail, only three feet wide

This painted rock reminds those who approach Baxter State Park and Katahdin of their responsibility to preserve the pristine qualities of this remote northern outpost.

Sandy Stream Pond in Baxter State Park is a popular stomping ground for moose in summer. The odds of a moose encounter are greatest near dawn and dusk.

Flowering water lilies on Compass Pond seem to point the way to Katahdin, but Maine's highest peak really needs no introduction.

at times, provides the park's, and perhaps New England's, greatest hiking challenge. Hikers should prepare physically and mentally before setting out inside Baxter State Park; conditions can be unpredictable, and venturing off marked trails is foolhardy even for the most experienced adventurer.

Back on the Park Tote Road, be sure to drive slowly past Abol Pond. This is a prime moose-watching spot, and stopped cars are a dead giveaway that one of the gangly beasts has been spotted. If you follow the turnoff for Daicey Pond, you may meet up with some very tired hikers. The Appalachian Trail, which begins 2,168 miles away in Georgia, ends here in Baxter State Park. For a less-exhausting expedition, canoe rentals are available at Daicey Pond, Kidney Pond, and, farther north, South Branch Pond and Trout Brook Farm; all are 2 miles or less from the main road. Another popular stop is Ledge Falls, where the swimming hole and natural granite waterslide on Nesowadnehunk Stream provide invigorating fun.

Many visitors enter the park, then reverse and return to Millinocket, so traffic thins out considerably the deeper into Baxter you venture. The road also narrows as the dense greenery creeps closer. You'll notice vegetation changes as the road climbs. When you finally reach the Matagamon Gatehouse at the park's northern entrance, have a camera handy, because this may be the dirtiest your car will ever be. Back on paved road again, civilization returns gradually, but there are still few retail outposts, even in the town of Patten, which is home to the Lumberman's Museum.

Though ample, if primitive, restroom facilities can be found throughout Baxter, "forever wild" means there are no gas stations, no food services, no running water, no electricity, and no shops inside the park. Stash the money you save on snacks and souvenirs in your savings account. You never know how much it might grow.

LAKES AND LOGS
AROOSTOOK COUNTY

ROUTE 30

From Portage, follow Route 11 North. When Route 11 ends, turn right and follow Route 1 through Fort Kent.

It's practically impossible to drive Maine's Route 11 from Portage to Fort Kent without finding yourself in front of or behind a log-hauling truck for a stretch. The forest products industry is the lifeblood of northern Maine's Aroostook County—an area larger than Rhode Island and Connecticut combined—but don't let the serene lakes and soaring birds fool you. The timber riches of this region sparked much squabbling in the seventeenth and eighteenth centuries, and the modern-day Route 11 essentially follows a former battle road.

Northern Maine was once part of a French colony called Acadia, meaning "land of happiness," which also encompassed Nova Scotia, Prince Edward Island, and New Brunswick. There was no happiness shared between the English and French, however, who sparred over Acadia from the 1600s up until 1760, when France relinquished its North American holdings. The French influence was harder to dispel. French-Acadian culture is still preserved and celebrated in northern Maine, and in the 2000 census, 23 percent of Mainers identified their ethnic origin as either French or French Canadian. Portage, where this drive begins, is a French word meaning "to carry a boat and supplies over land between two bodies of water." The body of water you'll see off to the left is Portage Lake, a 2,471-acre coldwater fish habitat.

Prized cedar, spruce, and white pine forests were again at the heart of a territorial dispute that erupted in 1839, as England and the United States sought to define Maine's northern border. Ten thousand militiamen were dispatched by Congress to northern Maine, and as they marched through Aroostook County, the men felled trees and positioned them side by side, creating the "corduroy road" that is now Route 11. The Aroostook War was concluded by a treaty in 1842 without a single battle fatality.

Your shocks and your jawbone will be grateful that while Route 11 is still a logging road, it's no longer a log road. Drive slowly anyway, as this is definitely moose country, and the forests provide camouflage for the hulking creatures. The forests also provide a deep emerald backdrop against which purple, pink, and white clusters of wild lupines radiate each June.

Like Portage Lake, Eagle Lake is part of the Fish River chain of lakes. An industrious mill town thrived on the banks of the 18-mile, L-shaped basin as the twentieth century dawned and the Fish River Railroad was established, but the lumber and shingle mills have since been replaced by private vacation homes and sporting lodges. Eagle Lake is a popular area for hunting and trapping, snowmobiling and cross country skiing, boating and fishing. Human swimmers won't find the icy waters as inviting as the salmon and trout do.

As you close in on Fort Kent, bilingual signs and Eiffel Tower lawn ornaments will start to appear, and French ballads will emanate from the radio. At the end of Route 11, turn right and follow Route 1 along the banks of the St. John—the narrow river that physically separates Maine from Canada. The St. John River Valley was settled in 1829 by French Acadians deported from Nova Scotia by the English. The town's name, however, was derived from the blockhouse erected at the confluence of the Fish and St. John Rivers by a Maine civil posse sent to defend American interests during the "Bloodless Aroostook War." The blockhouse is now a state historic site and a National Historic Landmark, operated cooperatively by the Fort Kent Boy Scouts and the Maine Bureau of Parks and Recreation. It's constructed, of course, from cedar logs.

If you want to really log some miles, Fort Kent marks the very beginning of Eastern Coastal Route 1—which ends in Key West, Florida.

Aroostook County is the heart of Maine logging territory. This 1903 photo shows felled logs ready to be floated down the Aroostook River to the lumber mills. (Photograph courtesy of the Library of Congress, Prints and Photographs Division)

The sun is the only thing stirring as Portage Lake awakes.

Right:
The 50-mile Fish River flows northward, connecting a chain of lakes to the St. John River near Fort Kent.

Facing page:
Rolling grassland and wildflower meadows line this country road as it meanders toward Quimby.

INDEX

SUGGESTED READINGS

Beckius, Kim Knox. *The Everything Guide to New England.* Avon, Mass.: Adams Media Corporation, 2002.

Berman, Eleanor. *Recommended Bed & Breakfasts, New England.* Guilford, Conn.: The Globe Pequot Press, 2002.

Green, Stewart M. *Scenic Driving New England.* Helena, Mont.: Falcon Publishing, 1997.

Hobbs-Olson, Laurie. *Discovering Acadia: An Introduction to the Park and Its Environment.* Charlottesville, Va.: Elan Publishing, 2000.

Kavanagh, James. *New England Birds.* Chandler, Ariz.: Waterford Press, 2001.

Long, Tom. *New England Nature Watch: A Month-by-Month Guide to the Natural World Around Us.* Beverly, Mass.: Commonwealth Editions, 2003.

Marcus, Jon, and Susan Cole Kelly. *Lighthouses of New England.* Stillwater, Minn.: Voyageur Press, 2001.

Michelin New England Regional Road Atlas and Travel Guide. Greenville, S.C.: Michelin Travel Publications, 2003.

National Audubon Society Field Guide to New England. New York, N.Y.: Alfred A. Knopf, 1998.

Parsons, Greg, and Kate B. Watson. *New England Waterfalls.* Woodstock, Vt.: The Countryman Press, 2003.

Roberts, Bruce, and Ray Jones. *New England Lighthouses.* Guilford, Conn.: The Globe Pequot Press, 1996.

Struik, Dirk J. *Yankee Science in the Making: Science and Engineering in New England from Colonial Times to the Civil War.* Mineola, N.Y.: Dover Publications, 1992.

Thoreau, Henry David. *Walking with Thoreau: A Literary Guide to the New England Mountains.* Boston, Mass.: Beacon Press, 2001.

Agriculture remains a vital part of New England's economic and cultural life. Aroostook County, Maine, is the only place in the United States where schools still close in the fall to allow students to help with the harvest.

ABOUT THE AUTHOR AND PHOTOGRAPHER

A native of New York's Hudson Valley, Kim Knox Beckius has always enjoyed exploring neighboring New England. In 1996, she relocated to Connecticut and gained a more central "catbird seat" from which to observe and explore the region. Since 1998, she has produced About.com's New England for Visitors Web site (http://gonewengland.about.com), taking Internet users on a virtual tour of New England, providing lively, weekly commentary on travel and events, and sharing insight into Yankee tradition, history, and ingenuity. She is the author of *The Everything Guide to New England*, a comprehensive travel guidebook to the region. Her writing and photography have also been featured on several other travel-related Web sites and in magazines such as *Grace Ormonde's Wedding Style* and *Bride & Groom*. Much of the research for *Backroads of New England* was completed while Beckius and her husband, Bruce, were expecting their first child, Lara, who was born an experienced backroads traveler.

William H. Johnson is a native New Englander who lives in the Lakes Region of New Hampshire with his wife, Marilyn, and their cat, Mittens. For thirty years, his artistic landscapes have captured the spectacular New England countryside in all seasons. Johnson enjoys spending countless hours seeking images, sometimes visiting a place many times until the light and conditions are "just right." His photographs have appeared in numerous magazines, calendars, cards, exhibits, and advertising campaigns in New England and beyond. He studied photography at the Layton School of Art and Design in Milwaukee, Wisconsin, and the Doscher Country School of Photography in South Woodstock, Vermont. He was named Photographer of the Year by the New Hampshire Professional Photographer's Association and has earned several court of honor awards. Johnson's camera gear includes a Medium Format Mamiya RZ 67, a Large Format Arca Swiss 4 x 5 view camera, and the Fuji 617 for panorama shots. His film of choice is Fuji Velvia.